Scotland's leading educational publishers

National 4 & 5
PHYSICAL EDUCATION
COURSE NOTES

N4 & 5 PHYSICAL EDUCATION COURSE NOTES

Caroline Duncan • Linda McLean

© 2014 Leckie & Leckie Ltd
Cover image © Shutterstock/terekhov igor

001/24012014

10 9 8 7 6 5 4 3

ISBN 9780007504770

Published by
Leckie & Leckie Ltd
An imprint of HarperCollins*Publishers*
Westerhill Road, Bishopbriggs, Glasgow, G64 2QT
T: 0844 576 8126   F: 0844 576 8131
leckieandleckie@harpercollins.co.uk   www.leckieandleckie.co.uk

Special thanks to
Jill laidlaw (copy edit); Roda Morrison (proofread); Helen Bleck (proofread); Ink Tank (cover design); Jouve (layout)

Printed and bound by CPI Group (UK) Ltd, Croydon, CR0 4YY

A CIP Catalogue record for this book is available from the British Library.

Acknowledgements
Leckie & Leckie would like to thank the following copyright holders for permission to reproduce their material:
P14–15 AFP/Getty Images; P20 information on Kini Qereqeretabua's bleep test score from *Fiji Times*; P21 information on the average distances run in different sports from www.tribesports.com; P22 Cooper test norms from www.brainmac.co.uk; P32 information on Samuel Groth's serve from Guinness World Records; P41 (t) Getty Images, (m) Getty Images, (b) Getty images; P42 (t) Richard Paul Kane/Shutterstock. com, (m) Pavel Shchegolev/Shutterstock.com, (b) Domenic Gareri/ Shutterstock.com; P67 AFP/Getty Images; P69 (m) muzsy/ Shutterstock.com, (bl) CHEN WS/Shutterstock.com; P89 Popperfoto/Getty Images; P99 Andrey Yurlov/Shutterstock.com; P100 Photo Works /Shutterstock.com; P101 AFP/Getty Images; P103 lev radin/Shutterstock.com; P133 Natursports/Shutterstock. com; P134 Mitch Gunn/Shutterstock.com; P135 (t) Natursports/ Shutterstock.com, (b) Photo Works/Shutterstock.com; P143–144 Fast-break drills from *Basketball for Women 2nd Edition* by Nancy Lieberman, Human Kinetics; P146–147 AFP/Getty Images; P151 (t) bikeriderlondon/Shutterstock.com, (b) Solovyova Lyudmyla/ Shutterstock.com; P152 Winston Link/Shutterstock.com, P153 Getty Images; P154 Sonya & Jason Hills creative commons 2.5, P156 Kaliva/Shutterstock.com; P162 Natursports/Shutterstock. com; P163 Aspen Photo/Shutterstock.com; P164 (b) Doug James/ Shutterstock.com; P168–169 Getty Images; P171 CHEN WS/ Shutterstock.com; P175 (t) Lilyana Vynogradova/Shutterstock.com; P181 Lawrence Wee/Shutterstock.com; P184 Mitch Gunn; P186–187 Getty Images; P191 Natursports/Shutterstock.com; P192 Chanclos/Shutterstock.com; P194 (t) Rena Schild/ Shutterstock.com; P199 Chris Hellyar/Shutterstock.com

All other images © Shutterstock.com

Contents

Introduction

Course content

When studying National 4 and National 5 Physical Education you will learn about your own performance and how it can be improved. The process you go through will ask you to reflect on what you already know from your study of PE and of the other subjects you have covered as part of your broad general education (BGE).

This book should allow you to learn about the **factors that impact on your performance** and will give you practical approaches to try to develop your performance.

Although the focus of the book is to help students complete National 5, all of the tasks should enable National 4 students to make their way through the course with some teacher assistance.

The National 5 course is broken down into two internal units:

- Performance skills unit.
- Factors impacting on performance unit (FIP).

Course assessment consists of:

- A single performance – a special or one-off event.
- A portfolio – a collection of evidence showing your learning throughout the course.

The single performance is worth 60 marks or 60% of your final mark.

The portfolio is worth 40 marks or 40% of your final mark.

Performance skills unit

You will probably cover many activities in your course. From these you will choose your two strongest activities and try to achieve a pass overall for these two activities.

Within this performance skills unit you will have to consider the following outcome and assessment standards.

Demonstrate a comprehensive range of movement and performance skills in physical activities by:

- Selecting and applying straightforward movement and performance skills, with some complex actions, displaying consistency in control and fluency.
- Demonstrating body and spatial awareness with clear patterns and rhythms.
- Working cooperatively with others.
- Using and applying straightforward techniques and composition or tactics safely and effectively.
- Making appropriate decisions and straightforward adaptations in response to a range of variables.
- Demonstrating consistency of movement and performance skills in a range of performance contexts.

Factors impacting on performance (FIP) unit

In this unit you will look at the impact of mental, emotional, social and physical factors on your performance. You will consider how to gather information on your strengths and development needs, how to develop your performance and, finally, you will have an opportunity to monitor and evaluate the performance development process. This book gives examples of the types of tasks you can use to help you complete this process.

Within this FIP unit you will have to consider the following outcomes and assessment standards:

Outcome 1

Demonstrate knowledge and understanding of factors that impact on personal performance in physical activities by:

- Explaining in detail two methods used to identify factors impacting on performance.
- Explaining in detail the impact of one positive and one negative factor on performance.
- Explaining two approaches to develop performance.

Outcome 2

Develop personal performance in physical activities by:

- Describing strengths and areas for development in a performance.
- Preparing and implementing a personal development plan containing clearly identified development targets.
- Selecting and applying two approaches to impact positively on a performance.
- Monitoring and recording performance development sessions.

Outcome 3

Evaluate the performance development process by:

- Seeking feedback from others.
- Evaluating the effectiveness of the personal development plan in supporting performance development.
- Evaluating progress based on all information gathered.
- Identifying and explaining future development needs.

How are the units assessed?

As you follow the course, evidence will be generated and marked by your teacher. This evidence will show that you have achieved all the assessment standards.

Course assessment

The course assessment examines what was taught in the performance unit and the factors impacting on performance (FIP) unit.

These will be assessed through:

- A single performance.
- A portfolio.

In the performance element of your PE course you will be required to take part in a special, **one-off performance**. This has to be more challenging than the kind of experiences you will have completed within your performance skills unit.

Your single performance assessment should allow you to demonstrate your best activity.

You will have to consider the three key areas that this performance will be broken down into:

- Planning and preparing for performance – this will involve thinking about what you need to do **before** taking part in your performance assessment. For example, you may have to think about the strengths and weaknesses of your opponent, the music you may use during your dance or even what type of warm-up is most appropriate for the performance. **This section is worth 10 marks**.

- Carrying out the performance – you will need to show a comprehensive range of movement and performance skills and be able to use your decision-making skills when applying these skills to your performance. **This section is worth 40 marks**.

- Evaluating your performance – this will involve looking back at your performance and thinking about what went well and what did not go so well. **This section is worth 10 marks**.

For the factors impacting on performance (FIP) for the course assessment you will be required to complete a portfolio. This will be completed in school and then marked by the SQA. It has three main sections:

- **Section 1**: Understanding factors that impact on performance. **This section is worth 8 marks**.

- **Section 2**: Planning, developing and implementing approaches to enhance personal performance. **This section is worth 16 marks**.

- **Section 3**: Monitoring, recording and evaluating performance development. **This section is worth 16 marks**.

The course assessment will look at the types of things you did to try to improve any of the factors you identified as impacting on your performance. This is very similar to the assessments you will complete in class time to pass the FIP unit. However, although the process in the portfolio is the same, you will be asked more detailed and different questions requiring you to show how you have applied your knowledge about performance development.

The course assessment will ask you to gather information as you go through your performance development process. As you work to improve your performance the data you collect, the approaches you use to improve the specific factor which impacts on your performance, the way you monitor the progress you make while training and the success you have as a result of this training are all areas which will be examined.

Your centre will agree with you which activity will be the focus of the portfolio. From there, as you carry out the development programme, you will be asked to reflect on how different factors impact on performance in different activities.

How to use this book

Your teacher will direct you to the chapters that are relevant to your particular course.

Try to read through the information and make use of the activities suggested to help you develop your skills, knowledge and understanding of performance development.

Some of the activities can be completed in a group and you will be able to complete others by yourself.

Use the feature boxes to guide you through the sections, which are common to all of the factors which impact on performance (FIP)

The aim is to help you develop your performance by using the knowledge and skills developed in the FIP unit.

That is:

  Improved performance

Features of this book

What should I already know?

Throughout this book you will see the symbol on the left when you are required to reflect back on learning you have completed in earlier years and in other subjects you have studied. This will help you build on skills and knowledge you have gained from your broad general education (BGE).

Activity

Tasks that reinforce important knowledge or help you apply the knowledge to other activities in the course. You will do these on your own or with groups to solve problems and develop a range of useful skills.

Make the link

This feature highlights links between the topic you are studying, topics in the book and other subjects you may be studying.

CfE focus

A section is included to show where the skills and experiences you are gathering fit within the curriculum for excellence.

Fact

Facts relating to the knowledge or skills you are focusing on are included – just for fun!

Check your progress

Short questions that test your knowledge of each topic.

HELP NEEDED	GETTING THERE	CONFIDENT
◯	◯	◯

Thinking skills in PE

All the parts of your course are designed to encourage you to become:

- Successful learners
- Effective contributors
- Responsible citizens
- Confident individuals

In PE your experiences taking part in activities which form part of your course and in the activities you do after or outside school will help you develop physical, emotional, mental and social skills. The processes you go through and the knowledge you gain will help you to complete all the parts of the internal unit assessments and the course assessments.

The range of thinking skills you develop will be common to many of your National 4 and 5 courses. This will help you to make connections between different subjects and to use skills in both familiar and unfamiliar situations. By doing this you can begin to understand different concepts and move towards being successful in all aspects of your learning.

It is important to understand that the thinking skills you develop while studying this course will challenge you to think. Sometimes you might only need to **describe** – give details about what something looks like. At other times you will need to **explain** – give reasons why something is the way it is. When asked to **evaluate** you are being asked to look at advantages and disadvantages and to assess or measure the progress you make towards developing your performance.

The words in **bold** in the previous paragraph are **command words**. They tell you what **type of thinking** you need to do to show your understanding of the performance development process.

Throughout your unit assessment and course assessment (portfolio) you will come across these command words telling you to do something with the knowledge you have. When you understand what these words mean you will be able to answer the questions well and achieve high marks.

Command word	What you need to do . . .	Example
Describe	Give details about what the performance looks like, an outline of the parts that are good and the parts that need attention.	'My arm was bent as I hit the shuttle.'
Explain	Making clear the main points, issues and reasons why and how performance might be affected by the factors or why you chose the approaches you did to help develop your performance or what you will focus on after you complete your development plan.	'As my arm was bent I could not hit the shuttle hard enough to make it travel to the back of my opponent's court.'
Evaluate	Make a judgement based on the evidence you collected about the progress you made when trying to improve your performance.	'My overhead clear was better after training as I could now push my opponent to the very back of the court more often in a game.'

Skills for learning, skills for life and skills for work

Within your PE course you will develop skills for learning, skills for life and skills for work.

Specific skills	Focus in PE
Listening and talking	You will be carrying out different roles while taking part in PE. Sometimes this will mean you have to listen to instructions from a teacher and other times it might be that a member of your group is explaining what skills are going to be included in a sequence. By developing talking skills you will learn how to communicate clearly with small groups, with a partner or even with a large group, giving feedback, instructions or in planning a task together.
Emotional wellbeing	The activities you cover in the course should help you identify your own emotions and feelings and those of others. In a practical sense, by being able to do this you can start to solve problems and build up a collection of skills which will help you make decisions while performing and help you adapt when things change in a performance situation. These skills help develop resilience – the ability to cope with change.
Physical wellbeing	Your physical wellbeing is a primary focus in PE in National 5. You will work to improve the condition of your body, your overall health and to increase awareness of what steps you can take to get and stay healthy.
Working with others	This is another key area in the National 5 course. You will get opportunities to work on your own and at times with others.In these environments you will develop leadership and cooperative skills. These will stand you in good stead when entering the world of work.
Applying	PE is a very practical subject. You will learn a lot of information about how to gather data on performance, how to develop performance and how to check the progress you make while developing the areas which require attention. This knowledge will then be used to help you solve problems relating to performance in different activities. These thinking skills will be used not just in PE but in many different courses in school.
Analysing and evaluating	By examining performance you will get the chance to develop skills that equip you to identify strengths and areas that need development. These skills can be applied to any area of your life and will ensure that you make judgments based on evidence you gather. This should make decision-making easier and when you evaluate the progress you make, you should see progress made in terms of the targets you set for yourself.

The four factors covered in this book

	1 The physical factor			2 The emotional factor	3 The mental factor	4 The social factor
	Physical and skill-related fitness	Skills	Strategy, formation and/ or composition			
Methods of data collection	Leger test	General observation schedule (GOS)	Match analysis	Personal reflections diary	General observation schedule (GOS)	Self-appraisal checklist
	12 minute Cooper test	Scatter diagram	Digital analysis	Emotional checklists	Self-reflection checklist	Etiquette checklist
	Performance timeline	PAR sheet	Coach feedback			Questionnaires
	Pacetracker app	Focused observation schedule	Personal reflection			Discipline record
	General observation schedule	Digital analysis				
	POOCH analysis	Coach feedback				
	10-metre sprint					
	Standing broad jump					
	Number of squats/press-ups in 60 seconds					
	Grip dynamometer					
	Sit and reach test					
	Goniometer					
	Groin test					
	Illinois agility test					
	T test					
	Alternate hand-wall throw test					
	Plate tapping test					
	Ruler reaction test					

	1 The physical factor			2 The emotional factor	3 The mental factor	4 The social factor
Factors which impact performance	Cardiorespiratory Endurance (CRE)	Nature of activity	Strengths and weaknesses	Happiness	Level of arousal	Peer group influence
	Speed	Skills classification	Roles and responsibilities	Trust	Concentration	Inclusion
	Strength	Skill and skilled performance	Performance conditions	Surprise	Decision-making	Etiquette
	Flexibility	Stages of learning	SFC fundamentals	Fear	Problem solving	Roles and responsibilities
	Local Muscular Endurance (LME)		Principles of attack and defence	Anger		Cooperation
	Agility			Confidence		
	Coordination			Resilience		
	Reaction time			Optimism		
Approaches to develop performance	Continuous training	Shadow practice	Adapting/changing SFC	Deep breathing		Team building activities
	Conditioning	Feeder practice	Practice sessions	Visualisation		Positive reinforcement
	Circuit training	Repetition drills		Mental rehearsal/imagery		Use of role models
	Speed training	Pressure training		Positive self-talk		Clarification and reinforcement of role and responsibilities
	Agility circuits	Conditioned games				
	Weight training	Opposed/unopposed games				
	Multi-directional running	Combination drills				
	Mirroring drills					
	Reaction drills					
	Stretching (passive, static and dynamic)					
Monitoring and evaluating	Leger test	General observation schedule	Match analysis	Personal reflections diary	General observation schedule	Self-apraisal checklist
	Diary	Diary	Diary	Diary	Diary	Diary

N4 and N5 assessment standards

Learning outcome National 4	Learning outcome National 5
1 Demonstrate knowledge of factors that impact on personal performance in physical activities.	1 Demonstrate knowledge and understanding of factors that impact on personal performance in physical activities.
2 Develop personal performance in physical activities.	2 Develop personal performance in physical activities.
3 Review the performance development process.	3 Evaluate the performance development process.
Assessment standards	**Assessment standards**
LO1 Demonstrate knowledge of factors that impact on personal performance in physical activities	*LO1 Demonstrate knowledge and understanding of factors that impact on personal performance in physical activities*
1.1 Describing a method used to identify factors impacting on a performance.	1.1 **Explaining** in detail **two** methods used to identify factors impacting on performance.
1.2 Describing the impact of two factors on a performance.	1.2 **Explaining** in detail the impact of one **positive** and one **negative** factor on performance.
1.3 Identifying a factor that affects a performance and describing an approach to develop this.	1.3 **Explaining two** approaches to develop performance.
LO2 Develop personal performance in physical activities	*LO2 Develop personal performance in physical activities*
2.1 Identifying strengths and areas for development in a performance.	2.1 **Describing** strengths and areas for development in a performance.
2.2 Preparing and implementing, **with some support**, a **simple** development plan to impact positively on a performance.	2.2 Preparing and implementing a personal development plan containing clearly identified development targets.
	2.3 Selecting and applying two approaches to impact positively on a performance.
2.3 Monitoring and recording performance development sessions.	2.4 Monitoring and recording performance development sessions.
LO3 Review the performance development process	*LO3 Evaluate the performance development process*
3.1 Seeking feedback from others.	3.1 Seeking feedback from others.
3.2 Reviewing the effectiveness of the development plan in supporting performance development.	3.2 **Evaluating** the effectiveness of the **personal** development plan in supporting performance development.
3.3 Reflecting on performance progress based on all information gathered.	3.3 **Evaluating** progress based on all information gathered.
3.4 Identifying future development needs.	3.4 Identifying and **explaining** future development needs.

SECTION 1
The physical factor

1 The physical factor: aspects of physical fitness

This chapter deals with all the physical fitness features that have an impact on your performance.

The features we are learning to identify and develop are:

- Cardio-respiratory endurance (CRE)
- Speed
- Strength
- Flexibility
- Local muscular endurance (LME)

In this chapter you will learn:

1. How CRE, speed, strength, flexibility and local muscular endurance can impact on performance.
2. How to gather information about these features.
3. How to prepare for performance development.
4. To understand and apply approaches to develop performance.
5. To monitor performance development.
6. To evaluate performance development.
7. To identify and explain future performance development needs.

What should I already know?

From your broad general education you will have become familiar with many of these aspects of fitness. This was part of the health and wellbeing (HWB) experiences and outcomes (4–25a). You will also have some experience observing your own and others' performances to try to identify areas of strength and those that are development needs (HWB 3/4–24a). Part of the work you will have done in class and perhaps in your own time will have been to try to improve the development needs. In the experiences and outcomes for HWB in your broad general education you will have had to try to sustain fitness across all aspects (HWB 3–21a). You will also have recorded your progress made as you worked and any improvements you were able to see after training.

At National 4 and 5 you will take these skills and knowledge and use them in different activities to increase and deepen your learning about performance development.

Feature of the factor: cardio-respiratory endurance (CRE)

CRE can be described as the ability of the heart and lungs to transport oxygenated blood to the working muscles during exercise. Much like an engine in a car, the heart is the body's engine. This engine has responsibility for getting the 'fuel' (oxygenated blood) pumped around to the parts of the body that require oxygen. Thinking again about the car, an engine that has been looked after will be able to do its job better. It is more fuel-efficient and tends to last longer. When we compare this to our hearts the same rules generally apply. A fit heart can get more oxygenated blood around the body with each beat and recovers to its resting rate much more quickly.

The cardio-respiratory system can be trained to become more efficient and therefore impact positively on our performance.

> **Make the link**
>
> In your broad general education you will have looked at the circulatory system in Science. This knowledge will help you understand how the oxygen gets to our working muscles when we exercise.

How does CRE impact positively on performance?

By having heart and lungs that are 'fit' you are more productive in any activity. This means you can run for longer and after these periods of running you are able to recover more quickly.

In a hockey game, for example, this would allow you to move up the field with the ball ready to give a pass to a teammate who might be getting into a good position to score. Good CRE would mean you would be able to do this for the entire match.

Another example would be a trampoline performance; when you are completing a sequence you need to maintain good height and position on the bed. With good CRE you are able to stay high, giving yourself more time to complete turns and somersaults and keep yourself near the centre of the bed for the whole performance. This would mean you would score more points.

How does lack of CRE impact negatively on performance?

If your heart and lungs are unable to provide you with enough oxygen to allow you to perform then you will get tired easily and be unable to give a strong performance for the entire activity.

In volleyball, for example, this might mean you find it difficult to keep constantly readjusting to cover for teammates going up to block in the late stages of a game. A good opposition would see the gaps you are leaving and would begin to tip the ball over the block into the space just behind it, which you should be covering. This would mean you would lose points.

In netball, poor CRE would mean your opponent could get away from you and receive passes or even intercept passes because you were unable to keep up with your marking responsibilities. Ultimately this would lead to your team losing possession and probably the match.

GO! Activity

Make a table of all the activities you do as part of your course.

On this table evaluate (judge) the need for CRE in each activity.

Here is an example:

Activity	My evaluation
Table tennis	We play short games in class. I can take my time when it's my turn to serve or even to retrieve the ball. Usually the games only last for about 5 minutes then we change opponents. This means I get a chance to rest between games and since I don't have to move around too much I seem able to cope.
Dance	Near the end of my dance performance I feel very out of breath. This makes it difficult for me to stay in time to the music when the dance speeds up as it comes to a close.

Your teacher might set up a range of activities or scenarios for you to try to get some experience investigating the need for CRE across a range of activities/sessions. For example:

- 10-minute basketball game
- 15-minute game of badminton
- Centre midfield position in hockey or football, where there is the need to constantly move.

Questions to be asked when activities are completed:

1. How did you **feel** near the end of the session?
2. How **successful** were you near the **end** of the session in **comparison** to the **beginning**?

CfE focus

Well done. By completing this task you are developing skills that will help you to become a **successful learner** – part of this includes work to assist you reflecting on action you took and then trying to work out if the course of action was effective or not. This means as you investigate the need for CRE within the activities you have covered in your course you will be required to think about the reasons **why** each activity needs CRE.

Skills for life, learning and work

Investigative skills – **comparing** a range of activities.

Evaluative skills – making **judgements** about the need for CRE within different activities.

✔ Assessment in PE

1.2 Explaining in detail the impact of one positive and one negative factor on performance.

You could make use of the knowledge you have learned in this section to help you explain how CRE can have a positive or negative impact on any performance.

How do I gather information on this feature within the physical factor?

The first stage in any performance analysis process is to gather information on your whole performance. This gives an accurate picture of what the whole performance looks like and makes sure **all** of the possible causes of a poor performance are examined. To do this we use a general observation schedule (GOS).

The general observation schedule should have criteria listed from a 'model performance'. This means you would compare and evaluate your own overall performance to that of a successful, ideal version.

An example of a GOS is included on page 32.

Having looked at your whole performance by using this general observation schedule and identified that the physical factor is an area you need to investigate further, you will then have some evidence about what your whole performance looks like and how CRE impacts on it positively or negatively.

In most activities this will require you to use a general observation schedule with timescales added to it. This will allow you to examine how your performance changes as it progresses. You will need to look at all aspects involved in the activity to try to assess if CRE affects the kind of things you need to do within the performance. For example, what happens to your shooting in netball when you begin to tire in the last quarter of a 60-minute game?

GO! Activity

You could also use a graphic organiser to help you identify the changes you observe as your performance comes to an end. Get an observer to complete this for you or to video your performance and then watch it while completing the organiser.

Insert a timeline for the period of time your activity lasts.

Performance Timeline

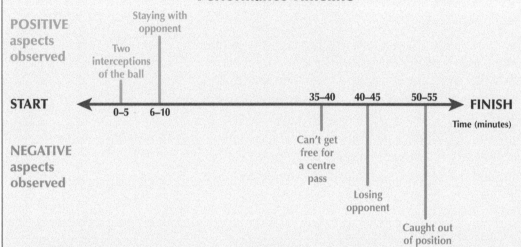

You could also make use of the variety of apps, for example Pacetracker, which are available to give factual information about how your running changes as your performance continues. These then calculate your average distance covered throughout a whole game. You could perhaps compare your averages with others in your class who are more consistent players, or even look at the average distances model performers in your activity cover in an entire match. This would give you a clear indication of how CRE affects your ability to keep running throughout an activity. Tennis players can cover over 4 km in a match, whereas footballers and rugby players can sometimes achieve distances of over 11km in a full match.

✗ Fact

There are unconfirmed reports that David Beckham has completed all 23 levels of the bleep test.

Fiji's rugby star Kini Qereqeretabua achieved 17.1 in the bleep test in January 2007.

Having first looked at your whole performance you may have noticed deterioration as the activity progressed. You could now focus or zoom in to measure how good or how poor your CRE actually is. There are a variety of ways of doing this. You could use the Leger test (bleep test) or the 12-minute Cooper test.

Both of these are standardised tests. They have set rules or protocols about how they should be set up. This means they are organised the same way wherever they are used. The results they produce can therefore be reliably compared and they are likely to be accurate. This gives us a firm foundation when we begin to plan our programme of work to develop performance.

Activity

The Leger test

Set up an area and mark it out with two cones. Draw a line between the two cones.

Set the CD player up and follow the instructions.

As the test progresses, the beeps get closer together meaning the runner has to run faster, with less rest.

She must make the line before the next beep. If she misses the line on two consecutive occasions she is out. The last numbered beep is the level achieved.

start ←——— 20 m ———→

The Cooper test

Set up the Cooper test.

Run round the 400 m track for 12 minutes. Count the number of completed laps and the number of 10 metres you achieve in this time.

Compare to the following norms:

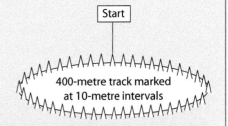

Start

400-metre track marked at 10-metre intervals

	Ages	Excellent	Above average	Average	Below average	Poor
Male	13–14	>2700m	2400–2700m	2200–2399m	2100–2199m	<2100m
Female	13–14	>2000m	1900–2000m	1600–1899m	1500–1599m	<1500m
Male	15–16	>2800m	2500–2800m	2300–2499m	2200–2299m	<2200m
Female	15–16	>2100m	2000–2100m	1700–1999m	1600–1699m	<1600m
Male	17–19	>3000m	2700–3000m	2500–2699m	2300–2499m	<2300
Female	17–19	>2300m	2100–2300m	1800–2099m	1700–1799m	<1700m

☑ Assessment in PE

1.1 Explaining in detail two methods used to identify factors impacting on performance.

You could use two of the methods described to explain the process you went through to collect information on how CRE affected **any** performance as it progressed.

You might also be able to use the information within your portfolio when you will be required to reflect on the methods you used to gather information on **your** performance.

Appropriateness of methods of data collection

The use of standardised tests allows performers to gather a picture of their strengths and development needs in as controlled conditions as possible. This means there is no opinion involved

✔ Assessment in PE

2.1 Describing strengths and areas for development in a performance.

You can use the results of the tests you carried out to identify areas of your performance that require attention. Give some details of your performance that allow you to be successful and then describe the things that go wrong because of poor CRE.

Again, this will assist you when you complete your portfolio. You can make use of this information to help you answer on the reliability and appropriateness of the methods you chose.

⁂ Make the link

There will be many circumstances where you will have your performance measured. In some careers performance will be measured by the amount of sales you make. In others performance will be measured against 'agreed criteria'. When your performance has been compared to the 'agreed criteria', strengths and areas for development are always identified. A programme of work or training is often then organised to help you improve your development areas. Check with the business studies department for some examples of performance-related pay. Can you see the link with the process we go through in performance development in PE and career-related performance evaluation?

and the result is as reliable and accurate as it can be. This issue of reliability is one that is crucial in the management of all tests or measurements of performance. It means there will be no errors that might give an advantage or perhaps a disadvantage to a performer when completing the test.

Preparation for performance development

Before embarking on a programme of work to improve our CRE there are a number of rules or principles we must consider. These can be remembered by using the acronym SPORT.

S is for **specific**
P is for **progression**
O is for **overload**
R is for **reversibility**
T is for **tedium**

These are the **principles of training**.

By using these principles we:

- Plan **what** we do in our training.
- **Develop the training** as we go along.
- Make sure the training is interesting and worthwhile, thereby positively impacting our performance.

The purpose of any training for CRE is to improve the efficiency of the heart and lungs. To do this we must force our bodies to do slightly more than they are used to doing. Each time this additional strain is put on the heart and lungs they respond by coping with the new workload expected of them and very quickly adapt to this new regime. Of course, if we ask too much of the heart and lungs by expecting them to cope with too big an increase in workload, the effects can be quite dangerous.

We **gradually** make the demands of our workload more challenging by working harder (**intensity**), working for longer (**duration**) or working for more sessions each week (**frequency**). This is called **progressive overload**. We also need to make sure we consider any changes we need to make to our training if for any reason we stop training. We lose fitness quickly (**reversibility**) and must reduce the training we do when we return after injury or absence. By keeping training interesting we prevent boredom and low levels of motivation while training (**tedium**).

GO! Activity

Copy out the graphic organiser below and complete the sentences in the circle. The first one has been completed for you.

Application of the principles of training

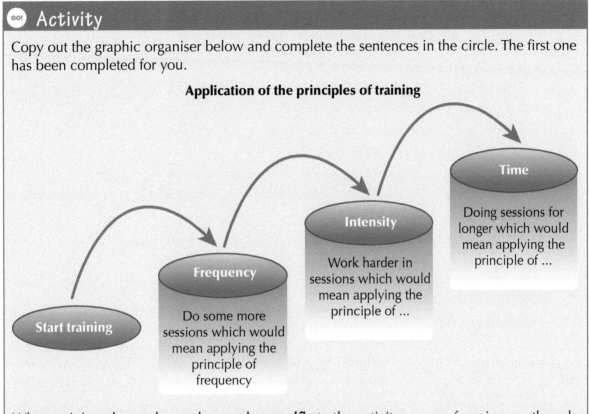

When training, the work you do must be **specific** to the activity you are focusing on, the role you have in that activity and the aspect of fitness you think needs attention. This means your training will be directed at making your CRE better for your chosen activity. The demands of the activity must be a consideration when setting up your training.

Progressive overload

When training, you must **progress** the work you do. This means making it a little more challenging as time goes on by **overloading** the workload you are doing. If you constantly did the same amount of training you would reach a **plateau** – a point where you would stop improving your CRE. Without progression your training would become unchallenging and probably boring.

When working to improve your CRE you must **overload** your training by increasing the **frequency**, **intensity** or **duration** of the training. By training more often, training harder or for longer, your CRE will continually improve. Even Olympic athletes apply this principle of overload, only in very small amounts.

There will be clear signs that it is time to overload your training. These might include finding the training too easy, recovering more quickly or just being bored with what you are doing.

GO! Activity

Look back at the activity table you completed earlier. Is improved CRE a requirement for effective performance in the activity you are focusing on?

Frequency

There are a minimum number of sessions you should train for each week in order to start improving your CRE.

Over a week, sessions should be organised to allow the body to recover from the training you are doing.

Therefore three sessions a week is the recommended starting point for improving this aspect of fitness.

GO! Activity

Copy out and complete the table.

How might your training week look?

Monday	Tuesday	Wednesday	Thursday	Friday	Saturday	Sunday
					Match day	

Can you explain why you have arranged your training this way?

📌 Fact

Cyclist Miguel Indurain has recorded a resting heart rate of 28 beats per minute. This does not beat the world record for a healthy heart. Martin Brady had his resting heart rate recorded at 27 beats per minute in 1969.

Make the link

In food technology and science you will look at digestion and how the body reacts when it eats. The knowledge you have from these subjects should help you explain the changes in your heart rate.

Intensity

While training to improve your CRE, measuring how hard you are working is crucial. This is the principle of **intensity**. We do this by checking our pulse. Our heart has a resting heart rate of somewhere around 60–100 beats per minute. Everyone is different. A low heart rate often indicates a fit and healthy heart.

GO! Activity

Find your pulse. Carefully count how many beats you feel in a minute. Keep a record of this. Tomorrow morning, before you get out of bed, check it again. This number is more likely to be your accurate resting heart rate. Check it at intervals throughout the day. For example how does it change after you've eaten? How does it change before you sit a test in Science, for example? Can you explain why it changes even when you are not exercising?

There is a 'zone' within which your heart must stay while developing your CRE. This is called your training zone. When we calculate this zone there are a few numeracy tasks we need to complete.

Step 1: Subtract your age from 220. This is your **maximum heart rate**.

Step 2: Find 60% of this maximum heart rate. This is your **lower limit**.

Step 3: Find 80% of this maximum heart rate. This is your **upper limit**.

When training, you must keep your heart rate between these two limits.

Try using a pulse meter or the Heart Rate 2.0 app to measure your heart rate as you exercise.

Another way of monitoring how hard you are working is by using your own internal feedback. This is sometimes called **biofeedback**. As you exercise you can judge for yourself the intensity of the work you are doing and divide it up into different levels. This is called **perceived level of exertion** (Borg Scale of Exertion). This involves you thinking about how you **feel** while you exercise.

GO! Activity

Using your own words, try to describe the different levels of exertion (tiredness) you feel while you exercise. Make up your own 10-point scale using words or pictures to describe the different feelings you have as you work harder for longer.

For example:

Level 1: I feel comfortable and could keep this pace going for a long time. I can talk easily as I work.

What would be your **Level 10**? This would be the maximum you could do.

How would you describe how this feels?
Can you keep it going for a long time?
Can you talk as you work?

Duration

Now that we understand about monitoring how hard you need to work as you train, we need to look at the length of time each training session should last. This is called the principle of **duration**. For CRE the minimum amount of time you should train in your training zone is 20 minutes. If a training session is shorter than this it might not be long enough to force your heart and lungs to adapt (get fitter). As you progress your training you can increase the amount of time you train for. This should be done in small steady steps, e.g. from 20 minutes to 25 minutes.

We now have the tools to improve our CRE.

✔ Assessment in PE

2.2 Preparing and implementing a personal development plan containing clearly identified development targets.

You will be assessed as you carry out your development programme. By being able to apply these principles to the work you do your teacher will be able to make sure you understand how to implement a successful plan.

Approaches that impact positively on performance

There are many approaches or methods of training you can use to improve your CRE. Running is a good approach and can be easily organised to suit the demands of the activity you are focusing on. Looking back at the activity table you completed earlier you should be able to identify the types of running that are involved in your activity. For example, do you need to be on the move all the time at a steady pace? Or are there bursts of intense running where you must get from one area to another as quickly as possible? By identifying what is involved in an activity we can 'match up' running training to **mirror** these demands. This means the training is **specific** and therefore is likely to have a positive impact on CRE within our activity.

Interval training

Interval training is a very useful approach to improve CRE for lots of different activities. It is organised to give 'intervals of rest' after periods of running/swimming/cycling. This rest period gives the heart and lungs time to recover but should mean the heart rate does not fall out of the training zone. The rate at which your heart recovers from exercise differs from person to person and is dependent on how fit your heart actually is.

GO! Activity

Run for a period of 10 minutes. You should try to push yourself hard enough to get out of breath. As soon as you finish running complete the chart below.

My resting heart rate is...beats per minute.

Time	Beats per minute
Immediately on stopping running	
1 minute after stopping	
2 minutes after stopping	
3 minutes after stopping	
4 minutes after stopping	
5 minutes after stopping	
6 minutes after stopping	
7 minutes after stopping	
8 minutes after stopping	

How long did it take your heart to return to near its resting rate? ...minutes.

The quicker your heart returns to its resting rate the fitter it is. This indicates your heart can work efficiently, getting oxygen around your body and also picking up the waste materials produced as a result of exercise.

An example of **interval training** might include running round a 400-metre track.

Ten fast runs over 40 metres with 2 minutes of rest between each run

GO! Activity

Work in a small group and compare the different recovery rates of the group. Present the average rate of recovery in a variety of different formats.

Make the link

In maths, science and business information you learn a range of different ways to present data. Use these skills in this task to make an interesting display of the class and group averages.

This method of training is very useful as it 'mimics' or copies the kind of running you might need to do in your activity where there is the opportunity to recover. For example, in football after a goal is scored the midfield player has time to walk back to the halfway line before the game is restarted.

Continuous running/cycling/swimming

Another method of training useful for developing CRE is continuous training. This can take the form of running, cycling, rowing or even swimming. The aim is to keep a steady pace for the entire period of training. The heart rate must stay in the training zone and care needs to be taken that the training is overloaded regularly to ensure improvements are made.

Conditioning training

This is another very useful type of training. It allows skills from the activity you are focusing on to be incorporated into activities that keep your heart rate in its training zone. It can also benefit the development of some of the **skill-related features** we will cover in the next chapter such as agility, coordination and timing. The skills a performer needs in the activity are also used e.g. dribbling in basketball. This means game skills are being developed at the same time as CRE and skills related aspects of fitness. For these reasons it can save a lot of time when a performer is trying to fit training sessions into a busy life, because conditioning can have a positive impact on physical and skill-related fitness and game skills through the same training programme. Conditioning training is usually set up by organising a group of 'stations' where the performer can work for around one minute before moving on to the next station. It is wise to start off with around six stations, do each for one minute and go round each three times.

Conditioning training can be really good fun as you can organise it to work with friends and to include elements of competition to keep it interesting and challenging. This is one of the areas you report back on when evaluating the effectiveness of your personal development plan.

You can design these stations for yourself and as long as you obey the principles of training you will see the positive impact of this approach.

Numeracy focus

If we do all six stations for one minute = six minutes. This would be a **set**.

If we do three **sets** of each of the stations that would mean we were working for 18 minutes.

Although this is just short of the necessary 20-minute minimum for improving CRE, with 30 seconds rest in between each station we can meet these requirements as long as our heart rate does not fall below the training zone.

Make the link

As part of your BGE you will have used some of these methods when developing your CRE. Be aware the knowledge you already have will be useful as you begin to work on your development needs.

GO! Activity

Can you calculate how long this training session will last, including all rest periods?

Can you explain why the rest period is needed?

Can you explain why we need to keep the rest period fairly short?

GO! Activity

Step 1: Make a graphic organiser for the activity you want to organise conditioning training for. Write the activity name in the centre.

Step 2: Identify all the skills required in that activity. Here is an example (for hockey):

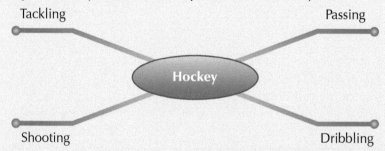

Step 3: Choose one or more skill and design a station where you would be on the move at all times using this skill, e.g. dribbling in and out of cones then attempting a lay-up at the goal.

Step 4: Present the plan for this station in the form of a poster for the rest of the class to follow. This must include clear instructions about the skill you are focusing on and provide a clear plan of what is to be done. You might want to video someone doing the station and then talk the group through the visual demonstration of your idea. Or make use of the Coach's Eye App to film the drill and overlay the commentary and instructions for others to watch on an iPad or laptop computer.

Step 5: As a group, choose six stations you want to include in your conditioning training programme. Set them up, try them, then apply the principles of training as you work through this programme.

Principles of training summary: CRE

Frequency	Intensity	Duration	Progressive overload	Specificity
Three times a week	60–80% of maximum heart rate	20 mins	Increase length of training session, cut rest periods, cover same distances in shorter periods of time.	Try to include types of movements, pace of movement as is required in focused activity.

✔ Assessment in PE

1.3 Explaining two approaches to develop performance.

You may wish to use the information included in this section to help you explain two of the approaches that are available to help improve CRE.

2.3 Selecting and applying two approaches to impact positively on a performance.

For this assessment standard you can actually make use of the approaches you investigated to help you develop your performance. You will need to demonstrate how you used this knowledge within your own programme of work.

This will also be useful when adding to your portfolio when you will need to explain your choice of approaches included in your programme of work.

Monitoring and evaluating

By keeping a diary where training completed is recorded, progress can be observed. This acts as an aid to forward planning and helps make sure training is increased gradually and sensibly.

The process of monitoring occurs **while** you are training and evaluation **after** you finish training. The evaluation is concerned with whether the training you planned and put in place actually worked and what next steps you would need to take to keep on improving. This process always involves revisiting your original methods of collecting data on your whole performance and comparing the results you gathered when you finish your development programme.

See Chapter 8 **Monitoring and evaluating** for further information and examples.

GO! Activity

The latest technology in electronic data collection is now widely available.

You might want to investigate the range of apps, e.g. Pacetracker, you could use to monitor the work you complete and the targets you set yourself for improvement.

Make the link

The skills you have learnt in this area of your course will stand you in good stead in many other areas of life. By taking responsibility for examining your performance, identifying areas which require attention, and then planning and taking some action to overcome these development needs, you have learnt useful problem solving techniques. These can be applied to areas of study where there is a need to find a solution to an area of difficulty. Where else in your studies do you follow this same process? Make a list.

✔ Assessment in PE

2.3 Monitoring and recording performance development session.

By providing evidence of the work you completed while training you will achieve this standard. You might want to use the methods included in Chapter 8 **Monitoring and evaluating** to record your training sessions.

Within your portfolio the process of monitoring will also be examined.

GO! Activity

Get a coach/partner/observer to complete the second version of your whole performance analysis and compare the two records.

Check your progress

Complete the following to check your understanding of this chapter.

	HELP NEEDED	GETTING THERE	CONFIDENT
1. Describe the impact of good CRE on your performance.	◯	◯	◯
2. Describe how we would gather information about the effectiveness of your CRE when performing.	◯	◯	◯
3. Explain what you understand about the principles of training.	◯	◯	◯
4. Describe how you overloaded your training.	◯	◯	◯
5. Choose one method of training and explain why it was effective in improving your CRE.	◯	◯	◯

Judge whether you were able to complete these easily. If not, go back and look over some of the explanations or speak to your teacher for further advice.

Feature of the factor: speed

Speed can be defined as the time taken to cover a certain distance. In sport and physical activity speed is a very valuable aspect of fitness. In swimming the faster the arms pull through the water, the better time a swimmer will achieve. In gymnastics the quick run up towards the horse will allow the gymnast to gather enough speed to help him rotate upwards, gaining full height and enough time to complete his vault. In some activities the fast movement of a body part is required to add power, making a shot more effective.

Speed is required to react to a signal or stimulus and begin to move – this is called reaction time. An athlete in the 100 metres race reacts to the starter's gun and begins running. A hockey player goes from standing still at a penalty corner to reacting to the striker hitting the ball out.

The length of your stride when you are running, the number of steps you take while running or the technique you use when trying to move your arm quickly, are all areas you can focus on to try to improve speed.

How does speed impact positively on performance?

Depending on the activity, speed can be used to great advantage in a competition against the clock.

● Activity

Class activity to complete a paper chase.

On a sheet of flip-chart paper or on a white board in the classroom, each person or team takes turns to add an activity that is affected by speed.

This could be the result of the activity or in parts of a performance. For example, one group might say an 800-metre race is decided by who passes the finishing line in the fastest time. The next group might say netball is affected by who can get out the quickest to receive a centre pass. Another group might say that the fast swing of the stick while lunge tackling in hockey could steal the ball and help a team gain possession to score.

	Activity
1	
2	
3	
4	
5	
6	
7	
8	
9	
10	

The purpose of the activity is to find as many examples as possible where the speed of the whole body or of a body part impacts on performance.

Looking back at the table of activities you created in the CRE section, you should be able to identify situations in most activities where speed is required. Being able to get to a ball first in a game, complete an event quickest or use fast movements to generate power would give you an advantage over competitors. A fast arm means a service is hard to return.

Make the link

You will remember from your broad general education that you have looked at parts of your own performance and tried to identify areas that require attention. In this next activity look back at the activities you completed and try to reflect on the need for speed.

How does lack of speed impact negatively on performance?

Having poor speed in your arm action when playing an overhead clear in badminton would almost certainly mean your shot would only reach the middle of your opponent's court. This would allow them to reply with a smash, probably winning the point.

Poor speed of rotation in your hips and shoulders when performing swivel hips in trampolining would mean you would be unlikely to get all the way round to complete your second seat drop. This would make your sequence look messy and most certainly lose points.

In volleyball, slow speed by the covering player to get to a tip from the opposition just over the block would mean the loss of a point.

✔ Assessment in PE

2.1 Describing strengths and areas for development in a performance.

By examining your performance and identifying speed as an area that requires attention, you should be able to describe the impact of this aspect of fitness on your overall performance. For example, how it limits or assists you to be a better performer.

Activity

From all the activities you know, choose one and prepare a poster showing how speed influences performance. You can label the poster with words or drawings showing when speed is needed.

How do I gather information on speed?

A general observation schedule (GOS) might have highlighted that the centre midfield player was not getting back quickly enough to tackle their opponent with the ball. This would indicate poor speed levels.

A GOS could have the following layout:

Activity: Football

Feature of a model performer	Always	Sometimes	Never
Sprint to get to 50/50 ball first			
Sprint forward to assist the attack			
Sprint back to get into position to defend			

Many tests for speed are organised around running a measured distance and recording a time. This simply tells you the time taken to cover a certain distance.

GO! Activity

Choose an activity that is part of your course. Think about the distance you need to cover while sprinting in this activity. You could use the Pacetracker app to help you calculate the distance and time taken to cover certain areas of the pitch/court or to calculate your average speed over the duration of the whole activity.

Choose your playing area. Press start. Watch the game. Put your finger on the screen exactly where the player was standing when he began the run. Move your finger to the place where the run finished. Press pause and the app will tell you what the distance covered was and the time taken to cover that distance. This gives you some data to show how effective speed is in a performance situation. This is a method used to identify how speed impacts on performance within the activity.

Now, with a partner, plan to set up a straight sprint test using the average distance you might need to sprint in your activity. Complete the following tasks so that you decide on the rules/protocols you need to put in place to make sure your test is accurate and reliable.

Draw out the way you will set out your testing area. This should include measurements you will use and how you will mark the start and finishing places. You should also make clear how you will time each participant and where the results will be recorded.

For example:

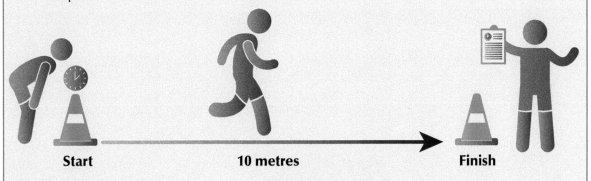

Start   **10 metres**   **Finish**

Instructions/test protocol

The participant should stand at the starting cone and when the starter calls 'go' should sprint to the finishing cone when the starter will call out the time taken. The results should be recorded on the chart, along with the date and the weather conditions if the test is conducted outdoors.

✔ Assessment in PE

1.1 Explaining in detail two methods used to identify factors impacting on performance.

By using your knowledge about the different ways to measure your speed you will be able to demonstrate your understanding of this standard.

☆ CfE focus

By developing skills while working together with others to complete a task you are demonstrating ability to be an effective contributor.

Make the link

When making choices about courses to study further you should base these decisions on your performance in the subjects you have studied. It would be unwise to choose a subject you found difficult and made little progress in ahead of one you find straightforward.

Appropriateness of methods of data collection

By testing using the length of sprint covered in the activity you are training for it is likely that when you retest you will be able to make realistic comparisons and judgements about the effectiveness of your programme of work. The results of your test will need to be trustworthy and reliable so that you can confidently say if your training has managed to improve your speed.

Whichever method you use, it is vital after training to use the same test to retest. This means you can easily look at before and after results to check for improvements.

Reliability is an important issue. Using these results to continue speed training would be a waste of time if the times were not recorded accurately. For example if the retest distance was 12 metres rather than the 10 metres of the initial test then the time taken would be greater than the initial test. This might lead the performer to think the training they did was ineffective, when in fact the retest conditions were not consistent. From the retest results decisions are taken about future needs so it is crucial the evidence is accurate.

Preparation for performance development

When planning a programme of work to improve our speed the same rules or principles apply as those we used when working on CRE. Remember we used the acronym SPORT.

S is for **specific**
P is for **progression**
O is for **overload**
R is for **reversibility**
T is for **tedium**

These are the **principles of training**.

By using these principles we:

- Plan **what** we do in our training to develop our speed.
- **Develop the training** as we go along.
- Make sure the training is interesting and worthwhile, thereby positively impacting, on our performance.

Again, we need to gradually make the demands of our training programme more challenging by working harder (**intensity**), working for longer (**duration**) or working for more sessions each week (**frequency**). This is called **progressive overload**. We also need to make sure we consider any changes we need to make to our training if for any reason we stop. We lose fitness quickly (**reversibility**) and must reduce the training we do when we return after injury or absence. By keeping training interesting we prevent boredom and low levels of motivation while training (**tedium**).

With speed the work you do must be **specific** to the activity you are focusing on, the role you have in that activity. This means your training will be directed at making your speed better for your chosen activity.

Approaches that impact positively on performance

Speed training needs to be high intensity. This means you are working near your maximum heart rate.

GO! Activity

Look back at the section of the book where you calculated your training zone. Do a new calculation for 85% and 90% of your maximum heart rate.

This is the zone you should work in when training your speed. This is close to your maximum heart rate.

GO! Activity

Set up a sprinting circuit to cover the distance you need to cover in an activity of your choice. For example, a footballer only really ever needs to sprint a distance of 2–20 metres regularly. This would be the sprinting distance for a footballer to work on. It would be interesting to build variety into the training circuit. You could do this by adding in different starting positions to encourage the development of agility and to train quick reactions when beginning sprinting. Try to make your sprinting circuit interesting and even add in changes of direction – as you might need to do in your activity.

You should make sure that you keep to the work-to-rest ratio of 1:5. This means if you sprint for 6 seconds, you must rest for 30 seconds before you sprint again. This gives your body time to recover and allows you to go 'flat out again' near your maximum effort ("intensly"). A reasonable starting place would be to do five sets of ten sprints with the required rest periods in between ("duration"). One speed session a week should be frequent enough to bring about the required improvements ("frequency"). Overloading can take place by increasing the length of sprints or doing more repetitions of the sprints – as long as the work-to-rest ratio stays the same.

Speed training programmes

Your training sessions for speed should take place **first** in an overall training session. This makes sure you are fresh and not tired from any other training you might be doing. If your sprint sessions are performed when you are not tired you will have the best chance to produce your maximum effort.

An example of a speed-training programme might be:

Get into groups of six and number each person 1–6. The following circuit should allow one person to work at a time while the others rest. This will make sure you have sufficient time to rest and then produce near maximum speed work.

Week 1: Sessions 1 and 2

Station 1: Weaving

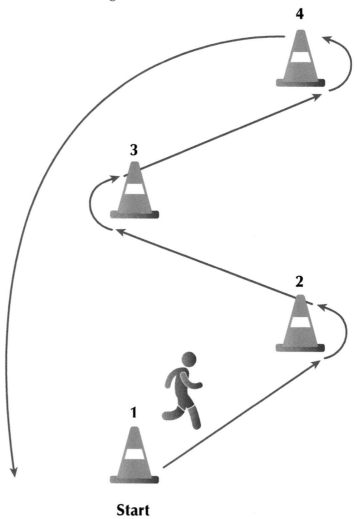

Start

Station 1

Start at cone 1 then change direction to 2, then 3 and after going round cone 4 sprint back to the start line.

Everyone does the sprint six times.

Station 2: Multi-directional running

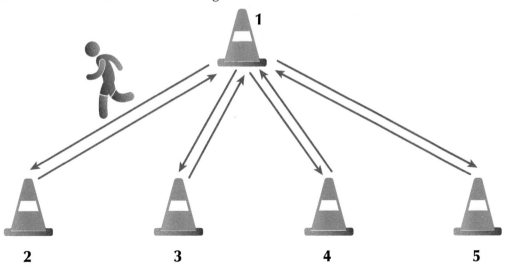

Station 2

Sprint from cone number 1 to 2 and back.
Then from cone number 1 to 3 and back.
Then from cone number 1 to 4 and back.
Then from cone number 1 to 5 and back.
Everyone does the sprints six times.

Station 3: Pyramids

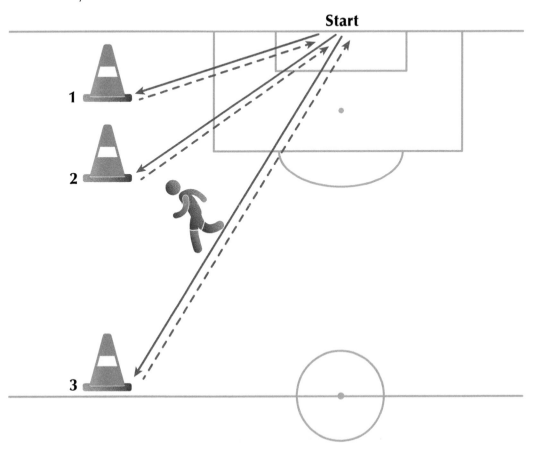

Station 3

Start at the goal line, sprint to first cone at 10 metres, then jog back.

Immediately as you return to the goal line, sprint to cone 2 at the edge of the penalty box, then jog back

Immediately as you return to the goal line, sprint to the halfway line, then jog back.

Everyone has to do the sprints six times.

Week 2: same as week 1 but add one repetition to each drill – now do seven of each sprint.

Week 3: add on another station – now do four stations of seven sprint repetitions, e.g. use the lines of the court in the game you are working to improve. Add cones at the corners to encourage fast, controlled backwards speed. Numbers could be called out in a variety of sequences to encourage the player to move to the front and the back of the court at different times.

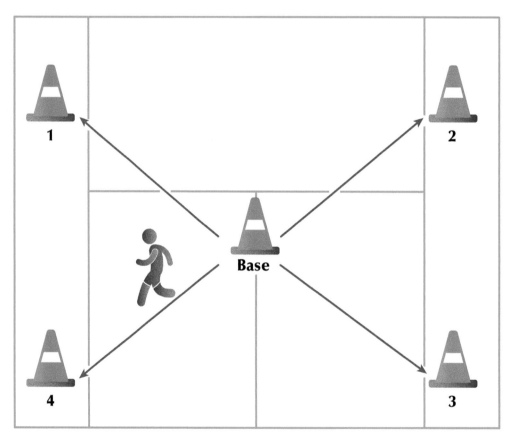

Station 4

It must be remembered that it is the **quality** of the speed work that is important. If not done at near maximum effort then speed will not improve –**rest** is important to ensure that the body is **able** to produce maximum speed.

Principles of training summary: speed

Frequency	Intensity	Duration	Progressive overload	Specificity
Once or twice a week	85–90% of maximum heart rate	10–15 mins	Add on another repetition or another station, making sure to keep the rest periods long enough for full recovery.	Sprint distances required for focused activity.

Monitoring and evaluating

Keeping a diary of training completed and progress observed is a good method of monitoring the work you are doing. There are many electronic methods you might like to experiment with for planning new targets and training sessions. You could make use of the Pacetracker app mentioned earlier in the book – or even invent your own mechanism. See Chapter 8 for examples of how you could monitor your performance development for speed training.

By using the Pacetracker app during a game it should be easy to see progress made working on speed. Changes you would expect to see in a game should be obvious. For example, in hockey you would expect to see a performer cover distances with the ball more quickly. A defender should be quicker to track back to close down the player with the ball. This should result in the player with the ball making an error, being dispossessed or having a pass intercepted because of being under pressure by the presence of the approaching defender. In badminton the time taken to get from the back of the court to the front should have reduced so the player can arrive in time to play the return.

Finally, it is necessary to look at your overall performance using an observation schedule. The observation schedule should examine times in a game where you lose possession of the ball because of lack of speed, times when you are unable to keep up with an opponent, cannot get out fast enough to tackle at a penalty corner or simply do not win a race. This will give you final proof of the effectiveness of your training.

✔ Assessment in PE

3.1 Seeking feedback from others.

3.2 Evaluating the effectiveness of the personal development plan in supporting performance development.

3.3 Evaluating progress based on all information gathered.

By comparing 'before' and 'after' performance data you should be able to see improvements that can be attributed to improved speed. You should be able to identify which parts of your overall performance have been impacted by improved speed.

Future needs

Decisions should be made about the usefulness of the training completed. Should speed be an aspect of fitness that needs to remain the focus of attention? Or is there another, more pressing performance problem?

✔ Assessment in PE

3.4 Identifying and explaining future development needs.

Your new performance levels should be an indication of whether speed should remain an area of continued focus. If so, you must be able to explain that by further increasing your speed you will be able to achieve better times if running or to get back even quicker to set up the zone defence in basketball to prevent the opposition's fast break strategy, for example.

Check your progress

Complete the following to check your understanding.

	HELP NEEDED	GETTING THERE	CONFIDENT
1. Describe the benefits of having good speed in your performance.	◯	◯	◯
2. Explain the process you would go through to gather information on your speed.	◯	◯	◯
3. Describe the type of stations you should include in your speed circuits.	◯	◯	◯
4. Explain why you must include long rest periods when speed training.	◯	◯	◯
5. Explain why speed training should be the first activity in a training session.	◯	◯	◯

Make a judgement – were you able to complete these easily? If not, go back and look over some of the explanations or ask your teacher for advice.

Feature of the factor: strength

Strength is the maximum force a group of muscles can exert in one movement. Strength can be broken down into three different types, **explosive**, **dynamic** and **static**.

The **explosive** strength Greg Rutherford used in his Olympic long jump final helped literally propel him upwards and forwards to win his gold medal.

In the swimming pool Ellie Simmonds' strong **dynamic** arm and shoulder strength helped pull her ahead of all the other competitors to win two gold medals and set a new world 400m freestyle record.

Daniel Purvis demonstrated pure **static** strength in the men's gymnastic rings competition. Holding this position requires the athlete to hold his whole body steady for around 3 seconds.

There will be a number of activities you experience which require each of these types of strength. In rugby static strength is required to hold the scrum steady and to stop the other team progressing forwards. In netball, when rebounding to collect a failed shot the goal defence uses explosive strength to drive up to get to the ball first. In tennis a player requires significant dynamic strength in the arms and shoulders to play out a long two-minute rally successfully.

GO! Activity

Create a player profile showing how each of the types of strength would help a performer be more effective.

Strength profile: basketball player

Static strength required to: hold position when setting a screen to block opponent from being able to dispossess teammate

Dynamic strength required to: repeatedly catch and throw over the period of a game.

Explosive strength required to: jump when laying up to get close to the basket to score. Power is generated to take the player quickly upwards towards the basket.

In creative activities the three types of strength allow a dancer to hold a supported balance with a partner without being pushed over. The dancer obviously would require to do jumps which were high and powerful and also when repeating certain motifs would be required to use dynamic strength to do the same arm or leg actions over and over again through the dance performance.

How does strength impact positively on performance?

All three types of strength are required in most activities to varying degrees – more static strength might be required of a hooker in rugby than by a hockey player perhaps.

Depending on the activities you are interested in strength could still be a focus for performance development. Being required to jump higher than an opponent (explosive strength), to hold off a defender (static strength) or to repeat strong movements over and over again (dynamic strength) to make it difficult for someone to return the ball/shuttle, is obviously an advantage.

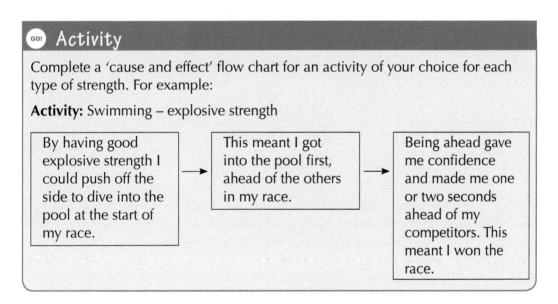

GO! **Activity**

Complete a 'cause and effect' flow chart for an activity of your choice for each type of strength. For example:

Activity: Swimming – explosive strength

| By having good explosive strength I could push off the side to dive into the pool at the start of my race. | → | This meant I got into the pool first, ahead of the others in my race. | → | Being ahead gave me confidence and made me one or two seconds ahead of my competitors. This meant I won the race. |

✔ Assessment in PE

2.1 Describing strengths and areas for development in a performance.

By identifying areas of your performance where strength is required you can describe the impact of strength on your activity.

⬦ CfE focus

By trying to analyse the impact of strength on your performance you are developing analytical skills that will enable you to become a **responsible citizen**. This means you are gaining experience in examining knowledge you have and evaluating the next steps you might need to take.

How does lack of strength impact negatively on performance?

Lacking the required strength can mean performance levels fall. It can mean you are unable to hit the ball hard enough, giving the opponent an easy return, or even that in a one-on-one situation you hesitate to put yourself in the correct position to block an opponent and so leave your defence exposed when a fast break happens in handball. In an individual activity such as badminton, lack of dynamic strength would show itself in lack of ability to push the shuttle to the back of the opponent's court. A wise opponent would exploit this lack of strength and force you to play the shuttle from the very back of your own court, knowing it would be unlikely you would put his/her shots under any pressure with your reply.

In volleyball, if a lack of explosive strength when jumping to block in one of the front court players were noticed by the opposition then it's likely this player would be targeted by the attack. They would constantly try to set to the area where this player was blocking. Lack of explosive power would mean this poor blocker would not be able to get up high enough quickly enough to block. Therefore the spiker would have an easy shot to play.

How do I gather information on this feature?

Within a performance, data associated with strength might be gathered by looking at the efficiency of things like successful blocking in volleyball or rebounds won in basketball or netball. The general observation schedule would need to include these criteria so that data can be collected first for the whole performance. For example:

Activity: Volleyball

Criteria	Often	Sometimes	Never
1st pass successful			
Setting successful			
Spiking successful			
Blocking successful			
Covering the block successful			

Although the GOS would not indicate which aspect of fitness was responsible for the blocking being unsuccessful, a future standardised test would be able to identify if strength was a development need.

The Grip Dynamometer standardised test will tell you the maximum force the forearm can exert.

How to set up the test

- Using the hand you use most often, grip the dynamometer as hard as possible to move the needle as far around the dial as you can.

- The score is recorded in terms of the weight you managed to achieve.

- Make three attempts and record the highest score.

The 'Standing broad jump' indicates the amount of explosive strength the legs can produce.

The performer should stand with their toes close to the edge of the trigger board and try to jump as far as possible with no run-up.

The performer should make three attempts at this test also, keeping the furthest distance as the score to be recorded.

You could also measure dynamic strength by counting how many squat thrusts or press-ups the performer can complete in 30 seconds.

It would be useful to identify the muscle groups used most frequently in the activity you are focusing on. Using this information, choose a test that suits you best.

Appropriateness of methods of data collection

By measuring the strength of a group of muscles used in your activity you are making sure the measurements you collect are specific to the performance. This means that after training you can go back and re-do the test to investigate improvements to your strength and most importantly to your whole performance. There really would be no point in getting stronger arm muscles if leg strength was your identified development need.

✔ Assessment in PE

1.1 Explaining in detail two methods used to identify factors impacting on performance.

If you can give details about the methods you used to tell you how effective your strength was, you will be able to achieve this assessment standard.

Preparation for performance development

When planning a programme of work to improve our strength the same rules or principles apply as those we used when working on all other aspects of fitness. Remember we used the acronym SPORT.

S is for **specific**
P is for **progression**
O is for **overload**
R is for **reversibility**
T is for **tedium**

These are the **principles of training**.

By using these principles we:

- Plan **what** we do in our training.

- **Develop the training** as we go along.

- Make sure the training is interesting and worthwhile, thereby positively impacting on our performance.

With strength training we again need to gradually make the demands of our training programme more challenging by working harder (**intensity**), working for longer (**duration**) or working for more sessions each week (**frequency**). This is called **progressive overload**. We also need to make sure we consider any changes we need to make to our training if for any reason we stop training. We lose fitness quickly (**reversibility**) and must reduce the training we do when we return after injury or absence. By keeping training interesting we prevent boredom and low levels of motivation while training (**tedium**).

The strength training you do must be **specific** to the activity you are focusing on, the role you have in that activity and the muscle groups you use most often. This means your training will be directed at making your strength better for your chosen activity.

Approaches that impact positively on performance

Weight training is generally the most effective way to develop all types of strength. It is organised around how many repetitions you do and how many sets suit the type of strength you are focusing on. The main approaches used are:

- Explosive strength – medium weights moved quickly with 6–8 repetitions in three sets.

- Dynamic strength – light weight with 8–10 repetitions in three sets.

- Static strength – heavy weights with only 3–4 repetitions in three sets. However, because of the dangers of injury, training for this type of strength is not recommended for young people.

Some schools have fitness suites where there are machines that can be set to light, medium or heavy weights. This enables you to keep an accurate record of which exercises you are doing to improve the muscle groups you are focusing on.

Another method is to use a strength-training circuit. This should be organised after identifying the muscle groups used most in the focus activity. Organise the circuit to work on alternate parts of your body, e.g. arms, then legs, then abdomen, then back. For example:

Arms: dumbbell curl – ten repetitions on each side, two–three sets with light weights.

Standing with feet shoulder-width apart, arms by side. Bring weight up, palm facing upwards towards shoulder.

Legs: tuck jump – ten repetitions, two–three sets. Begin with feet together. Swing arms up and bring knees to chest. As soon as feet touch floor on landing, drive straight upwards again without stopping.

Abdomen: crunches – ten repetitions, two–three sets. Lie flat on the floor with feet on the ground and knees slightly bent. Bring upper body up, touching the knees with the chest.

Back: back extension – ten repetitions, two–three sets. Lie on stomach with arms extended above your head. Lift chest off the floor and hold for three seconds.

Assessment in PE

1.3 Explaining two approaches to develop performance.

2.3 Selecting and applying two approaches to impact positively on a performance.

Using circuit training to develop strength is one straightforward way to develop strength. To pass this standard you would need to describe and explain the exercises you include in your circuit, and the number of repetitions and sets you complete, as well as giving an explanation of the order of the exercises you include.

Principles of training summary: strength

Frequency	Intensity	Duration	Progressive overload	Specificity
Three times a week.	Low numbers of repetitions with light or medium weights.	20–30 mins	Add more weights or more repetitions.	Work on muscles used in focus activity.

Monitoring and evaluating

A diary or training card is essential when taking part in weight training. You might find it difficult to remember each weight used for each exercise and the number of repetitions completed. Therefore, by keeping a record you can easily see the weights you need to use. This prevents injury. Also, it is very motivating to see the progress you make as you increase weights, repetitions or sets. Check Chapter 8 to see the methods you can use to keep a note of the progress you are making.

Looking back at your whole performance will allow you to identify changes due to increased strength. Is the number of occasions where you get up to block at the net increased? Is there evidence that you are winning more rebounds? This would all indicate that your training programme had positively impacted on your whole performance. By retesting yourself you should see that your test scores improve. By comparing your before training and after training data, you can check for improvements. This again makes clear if your training has been effective.

✔ Assessment in PE

3.1 Seeking feedback from others.

3.2 Evaluating the effectiveness of the personal development plan in supporting performance development.

3.3 Evaluating progress based on all information gathered.

By looking back at the changes between your first observed performance and those gathered after completing your training, you will be able to make judgements about what improvements can be seen. This is information you will need to record when working to achieve these assessment standards.

Future needs

Strength is an area that generally needs ongoing attention. A session of strength-training work is part of an all-round programme for most performers. Muscles that are well trained do their job more efficiently.

✔ Assessment in PE

3.4 Identifying and explaining future needs.

As with all fitness development work, future needs are often linked to the maintenance of the aspect of fitness. To achieve this assessment standard you would need to explain why strength remains an area you need to keep working on or to explain why another aspect of your performance was to become your next target area.

☀ CfE focus

Seeing the benefit of an ongoing training cycle and taking responsibility for being determined to continue to improve is part of being a **successful learner**. By monitoring closely the progress you make and the steps you need to take to keep improving you will develop skills of self-regulation and self-discipline. These will help keep you healthy all through your life.

Check your progress

Complete the following to check your understanding.	HELP NEEDED	GETTING THERE	CONFIDENT
1. Explain what you understand about strength.	◯	◯	◯
2. Name the three types of strength.	◯	◯	◯
3. Describe one test for measuring strength.	◯	◯	◯
4. Describe a method used to keep a record of the training you completed to develop your strength.	◯	◯	◯
5. Explain how improved strength can impact on your performance.	◯	◯	◯

Make a judgement – were you able to complete these easily? If not, go back and look over some of the explanations or ask your teacher for advice.

Feature of the factor: flexibility

Flexibility is an aspect of fitness that contributes to overall good health. A definition of flexibility would be:

The range of movement around a joint.

A joint joins two parts of your body together.

GO! Activity

Can you identify joints around your body?

- The ankle joint joins your foot to your lower leg.
- The knee joint joins your lower leg to your upper leg.
- The hip joint joins your upper leg to your body.
- The finger joints join your fingers to your hand.
- The wrist joint joins your hand to your lower arm.
- The elbow joint joins your lower arm to your upper arm.
- The shoulder joint joins your upper arm to your body.
- The neck joint joins your body to your head.

Label the different joints on the diagram on page 52.

Unannotated and annotated versions of this diagram are available to download from the Leckie and Leckie website at www.leckieandleckie.co.uk/n45physicaled

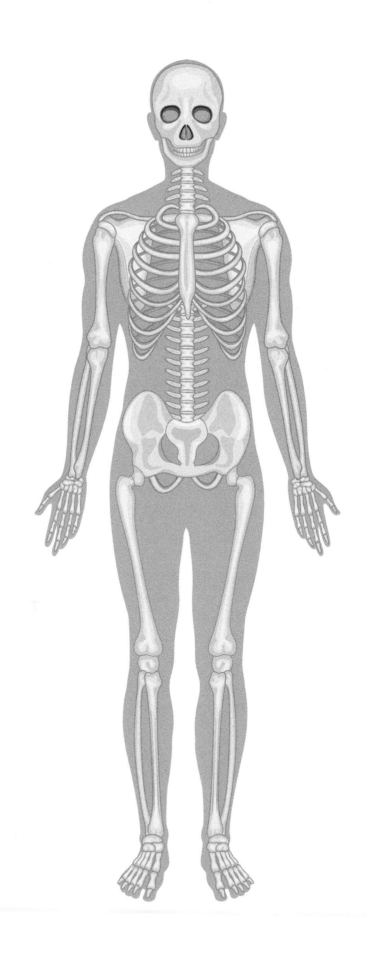

Muscle tug of war

Most of the joints in your body are involved in movements while you take part in physical activity. It is useful to have a clear picture of the main joints you use while performing. In this way you can identify areas where you need to focus in order to improve your performance in an activity. This also helps you to improve your flexibility when training.

The joints are held together with muscles, ligaments and a variety of blood vessels and tendons. When we think about our body's ability to be flexible, we are really focusing on the muscles that move the joints. Interestingly, the muscles work in **pairs** – one muscle makes the movement happen and the other muscle tries to stop it happening. A bit like a tug of war.

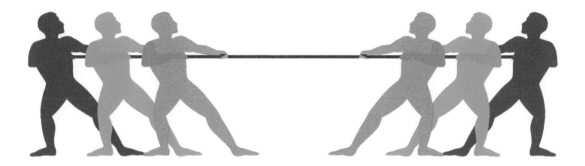

One set within the pair of muscles is called the **agonist** and the other set is called the **antagonist**.

Antagonists fight against something, trying to prevent some change of circumstances perhaps or trying to counteract the actions of another person or group.

When you compare this to the muscles in your body, one set wants to help you bend your arm but there is another set shortening at the same time, trying to counteract this happening. This is what holds the body in position, making sure our joints do not allow movements that could cause injury and damage.

At this point it is necessary to identify the main types of joints that exist in the body. There are four types of joints. These are:

- Ball and socket – found at the hip and shoulder.

- Hinge – found at the elbows and knees.

- Gliding – found at the ankles and wrists.

- Pivot – found at the neck.

☀ Make the link

In English, History and Modern Studies you will come across people who were called antagonists. These people tend to be adversaries or enemies of heroes. For example, Sauron is the main antagonist in the *Lord of the Rings* trilogy. In *Macbeth* the antagonist might be Macduff. In *To Kill a Mockingbird*, Bob Ewell would also be defined as the main antagonist.

From your experience of popular films, the Joker was Batman's antagonist and Robin Hood was the Sheriff of Nottingham's troublesome antagonist.

Activity

Using the diagram you completed earlier, try to describe the movement you are able to have at each joint.

Use a graphic organiser to give a description of the range of movements you have at your hips (see below), your shoulder, your neck, your knees and your wrists.

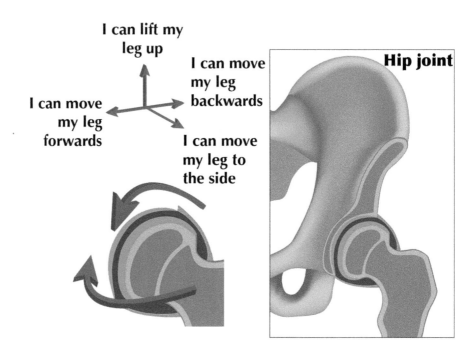

Later in this chapter we will try to measure accurately the amount of movement at some of the joints to get objective (factual) data.

When we understand the way joints work when we move, we can then look at developing muscles to allow increased movement and to improve our performance in a range of activities.

Make the link

There are examples of joints being used in other subjects you will have studied. For example, in woodwork a hinge is used to allow a cupboard door to open and close. In Information technology a ball and socket arrangement can be found in webcam stands to allow them to be repositioned and moved around easily.

CfE focus

By using your problem solving skills you are developing skills required to be an **effective contributor**. In this way you are learning how to look at problems and to try to use knowledge you have learned in a different situation to help you find solutions.

How does flexibility impact positively on performance?

Good flexibility allows performers to stretch without fear of injury in a badminton game, to raise the leg high into an arabesque position to make a dance look interesting and generally to make their movements more economical and effective.

Imagine you had to reach up to the top corner of a hockey goal to try to stop the shot from going in. Good flexibility would allow you to extend your arm high to do this.

In netball, the goal defence needs to have a good range of movement at her shoulder joint in order to get her hand over the ball at full stretch to try to make it difficult for the goal attack to shoot.

In tennis, service requires a great deal of flexibility at the shoulders to move the arm backwards in preparation for hitting the ball and then quickly forwards to put maximum pace on the ball.

In trampolining a routine will be awarded more points if the performer can bring his legs right up in front when attempting the pike position.

How does lack of flexibility impact negatively on performance?

Lack of flexibility could result in a performer losing points on a service, when an opponent has made him stretch to retrieve a shuttle played just over the net. In creative activities such as dance, gymnastics or trampolining, poor flexibility can make the performance look messy, uneasy and not smooth. This would lose the performer points.

Also, if the muscles around a joint are stiff and tight then injury can happen.

A warm-up is therefore essential.

> **Make the link**
>
> In some activities you completed as part of your BGE you will have looked at the impact of flexibility. This knowledge will be useful as you begin to look at other activities and start to measure your own levels of flexibility.

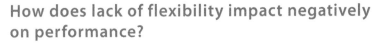

✔ Assessment in PE

1.2 Explaining in detail the impact of one positive and one negative factor on performance.

The impact of flexibility on your performance can be positive or negative. By using the information and activities on these pages you should be able to identify and explain how your performance is affected.

How do I gather information on flexibility?

Within the full performance it is necessary to pinpoint skills that were less effective because of poor flexibility. Then a more focused data collection is necessary.

For example, in badminton a scatter diagram may have highlighted that the overhead clear was a weakness in that it never reached the rear tramlines of the court. The badminton scatter diagram records where a shot lands. It could also be used, for example, to pinpoint exactly where the tennis service lands, or the place where a shot was taken from in basketball, or where the penalty corner was hit to in hockey. It records factual information about the position from where a shot was taken, where a pass or player is at specific points in a performance. This might highlight that there is some problem with your stroke, shot or pass. you would then need to focus in on each stroke, shot or pass in order to identify which part of the stroke, shot or pass is the problem. We do this using a PAR sheet.

Badminton: overhead clear

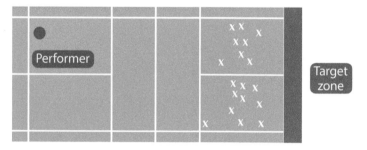

The PAR sheet might indicate that the arm was not brought forward from behind the head. This might indicate poor flexibility around the shoulder joint.

The PAR sheet records the three phases of any skill, the P – preparation, the A – action and the R – recovery. Roughly speaking the preparation phase covers everything we do **before** we hit, pass, jump, kick. The action covers everything we do **as** we hit, pass, jump, kick. The recovery phase covers everything we do **after** we hit, pass, jump or kick. Examples of PAR sheets for a chest pass and for an overhead clear are provided on page 57.

PAR sheet for a chest pass

Preparation (Everything you do **before** you release the ball.)	Satisfactory	Unsatisfactory
Ball held in both hands		
Fingers spread at each side of the ball		
Weight on back foot		
Ball held at chest height		
Ball close to body		
Elbows in		
Action (Everything you do **as** you release the ball)		
Push the ball forward, straightening arms		
Fingers extend in the direction of the pass		
Weight is transferred as you step forward		
Recovery (Everything you do **after** you release the ball.)		
Weight is back on balls of both feet ready to move in any direction		
Hands relaxed, ready to receive another pass		

PAR sheet for an overhead clear

Preparation phase	Satisfactory	Unsatisfactory
Turn side on		
Chasse to get under the shuttle		
Weight on back foot		
Non-playing hand 'sighting' (pointing at) the shuttle		
Racquet shoulder dropped		
Looking at the shuttle		
Action phase		
Racquet brought forward with speed from behind the head		
Weight transfers from back to front foot		
Shuttle hit with straight, fast arm		
Recovery phase		
Transfer of weight takes you forward towards base position		
Arm comes down and across body ready for next shot		

By using the PAR sheet, we can identify which part of the skill is the problem. We can also gather more specific data on the range of movement around the joints.

There is a range of standardised tests available to measure the flexibility of the main joints. These range from very scientific, objective measurement tests using a Goniometer, to others which ask you to stretch as far as you can and measure the distance you reached.

Skills for life, learning and work

A physiotherapist uses a Goniometer to measure a patient's range of movement before treatment. This gives an accurate starting point and provides a measurement that can be used to monitor improvements after treatments such as hip or knee replacements.

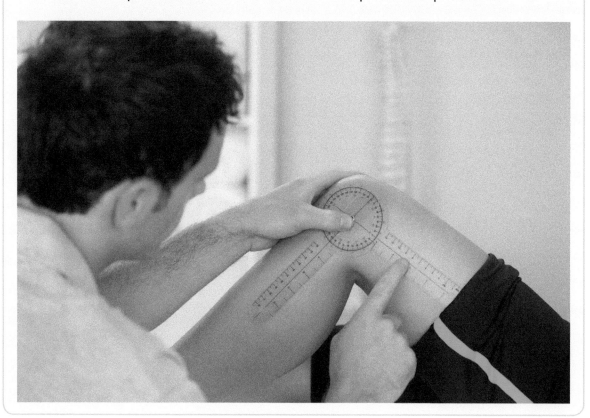

Testing flexibility

You might like to try the Goniometer for iPad app. This gives you accurate information about the range of movement around your major joints. However, you can also try the following more traditional methods. Try doing the following tests – being the subject and also taking responsibility for being the person who administers the tests. It is vital that you do a thorough warm-up before you attempt each test.

Sit and reach test

This tests flexibility **at the hip joint**. The following equipment is needed:

- Sit and reach box

- Ruler

- Recording sheet

Make sure you are warmed up. Sit down with your feet flat against the end of the box. Push the ruler as far along the box as you can, holding for a few seconds when you feel you cannot go any further. Have three seperate attempts at this. Record each of your three attempts. Keep the best score as your initial test result.

The groin test

This is another test for flexibility **around the hip**. The following equipment is needed:

- A measuring tape

Make sure you are warmed up. Sit down, put the soles of your feet together and measure the distance from your feet to your groin. Record the distance measured.

The rope test

This is a test for flexibility around **the shoulders**. The following equipment is needed:

- A piece of rope

- A measuring tape

Measure the distance from one shoulder to the other. Get warmed up. Stand with your feet apart with the rope held in each hand. Slowly lift the rope up and over your head with straight arms until both arms are behind you. Let the rope slide through your fingers as you do this so that you are comfortable at all times. Measure the distance between your two thumbs. Do this three times. Record each distance. Use the best distance as your rope score. Subtract the shoulder width measurement from the rope score measurement and then record.

☑ Assessment in PE

1.1 Explaining in detail two methods used to identify factors impacting on performance.

By using these tests and explaining how you used the method to identify the impact of flexibility on your performance you will be able to achieve this assessment standard.

These activities will also enable you to complete your portfolio for the course assessment.

💡 CfE focus

Having an awareness of scientific and medical techniques enables you to be a responsible citizen. This allows you to have an understanding of what might happen to you or someone close to you should they need surgery or be injured and require physiotherapy to aid recovery.

Appropriateness of methods of data collection

These methods of data collection are fairly accurate. However, human error can mean the results could be invalid. As the tests are 'standardised' – i.e. the way they have to be set up and carried out the same whenever and wherever they are used – this adds validity to the results you get. By being careful to set out the tests according to the protocol you make sure that each time you do the tests the conditions are the same. This means the results you get can be compared. If you do not set up the tests according to the protocol, then the results may not be valid.

🔅 Make the link

When you have your eyes tested the optician uses a standardised test using something called the Snellen Chart. Every time you have your eyes tested the same chart will be used. You will sit the same distance from the chart for every test and be asked to read from the top to the bottom every time. This enables the optician to see if your vision has improved or deteriorated compared to your last visit.

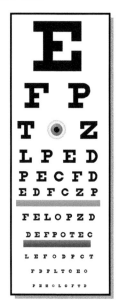

Activity

In these tests you will have been the subject (person doing the test) and the test administrator. In these two roles you will have had the chance to **carry out** the instructions and to be the person who had to make sure the instructions were **carried out** correctly.

In the role of administrator, what things did you observe subjects doing which meant the test was not carried out properly?

Complete the cause and effect table (one effect has been completed for you).

Cause	Effect
The subject 'flicked' the ruler instead of pushing it along the box and holding it in position when at full stretch.	She managed to get the ruler a greater distance along the box.
There was disagreement about where the measurement should be taken from for shoulder width.	
The subject bent her knees as she stretched along the box.	
The subject bounced then lunged forward to push the ruler along the box. She did not hold the ruler in position.	

Skills for life, learning and work

By using your thinking skills to investigate the problems you came across when doing these tests you are developing problem solving techniques. These will help you in many aspects of your life both in and out of school. If you can learn to question why something happens and what can be improved about a task you need to complete, then you will become an employable person.

Preparation for performance development

Before embarking on a programme of work to improve flexibility there are a number of rules or principles we must consider. These can be remembered by using the acronym SPORT.

S is for **specific**
P is for **progression**
O is for **overload**
R is for **reversibility**
T is for **tedium**

These are the **principles of training**.

By using these principles we:

- Plan **what** we do in our training.
- **Develop the training** as we go along.
- Make sure the training is interesting and worthwhile thereby positively impacting our performance.

With flexibility training we need to gradually make the demands of our training programme more challenging by working harder (**intensity**), working for longer (**duration**) or working for more sessions each week (**frequency**). This is called **progressive overload**. We also need to make sure we consider any changes we need to make to our training if for any reason we stop training. We lose fitness quickly (**reversibility**) and must reduce the training we do when we return after injury or absence. By keeping training interesting we prevent boredom and low levels of motivation while training (**tedium**).

The flexibility training you do must be **specific** to the activity you are focusing on, the role you have in that activity and the muscle groups that you use most often. This means your training will be directed at making your flexibility better for your chosen activity.

Approaches that impact positively on performance

Training for improving flexibility is a straightforward process and one where a performer can quite quickly see some positive results. This is done by organising a specific programme of stretching. These stretches should only be done after a thorough warm-up. This will prevent injury. Stretches should be held for around 5–10 seconds on each side of the body and the performer should be trying to gently stretch a little further each time or hold the stretch for one or two seconds longer each week.

Before we embark on developing our flexibility it would be wise to plan a warm-up. There are **three** stages to an effective warm-up.

Stage one would be any heart-rate raising activity, e.g. jogging or skipping. This gets the heart beating faster and so increases the amount of oxygen being sent around the body in the blood. It also increases the body temperature and gets the brain to begin thinking about what we are preparing to do. This should last around 5–10 minutes.

Stage two focuses on stretching the muscles and joints we are going to be using in the activity we are warming up to take part in. So for a badminton game, the big leg muscles would be stretched out, then the arms, shoulders, ankles and lower legs. By stretching gently in this part of the warm-up, the amount of

Fact

Daniel Browning Smith is said to be the world's most flexible man. Often called 'double-jointed', he actually has the same joints as everyone else but has an increased range of movement at his joints.

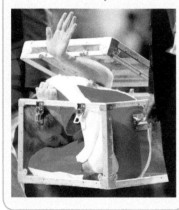

blood flowing into the muscles increases and the temperature in these muscles rises. This means the muscle groups are warm and are ready to work carrying out the movements involved in the activity.

Stage three of the warm-up involves beginning to do some easy skills that you will use in the performance you are preparing for. So in badminton you would begin an easy cooperative rally with a partner. In swimming a few easy lengths would be completed. In hockey some dribbling with the ball or easy passing practice with a partner would be done.

☑ Assessment in PE

It is useful to write down or record all the warm-ups you complete for the activities in your course. This will help you when you complete your one-off performance for your course assessment. A well-planned warm-up will get more marks.

Approaches to develop flexibility

There are three types of stretching training we will look at. You could include all of the same type in your programme, or try combining them to make your training varied and interesting.

Passive stretching

Working with a partner you, the performer, relaxes and let the partner move a part of your body gently until you instruct them to stop. For example:

Experiment working with a partner using a variety of stretches.

The benefits of this method of training are that you have the advantage of working with someone to help you improve your flexibility. It can really increase motivation and commitment to training if you have someone working alongside you encouraging you to continue to work hard. Communication and trust are vital when working with a partner in this situation. You must be able to tell them when to stop and they must obey your instruction or you could be injured.

Passive stretching can also be done on your own. You can hold your own arm or leg as you gently stretch.

Static stretching
Using your own body weight, simply take up a position and gradually stretch the muscle, holding it for around ten seconds.

Dynamic stretching

A range of exercises where the body part is moved, e.g. swinging your arm or leg. Do 6–10 times on each side of the body.

🔵 GO! Activity

Construct a programme of stretches to help develop the flexibility of the main muscles and joints used in an activity of your choice. You could use some of the stretches below or devise your own. Organise in a table or a graphic organiser.

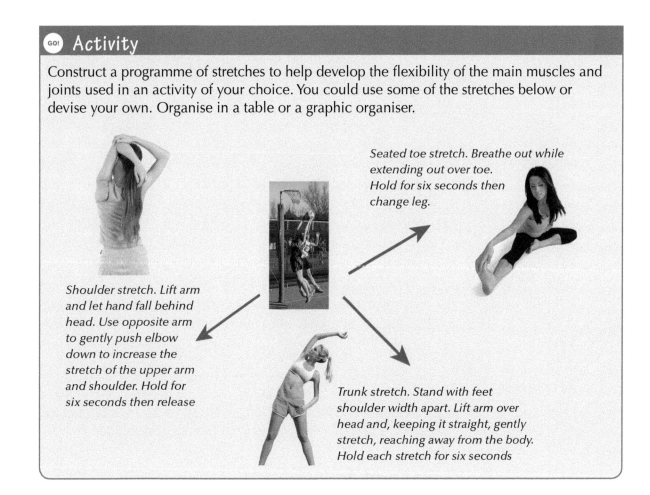

Seated toe stretch. Breathe out while extending out over toe. Hold for six seconds then change leg.

Shoulder stretch. Lift arm and let hand fall behind head. Use opposite arm to gently push elbow down to increase the stretch of the upper arm and shoulder. Hold for six seconds then release

Trunk stretch. Stand with feet shoulder width apart. Lift arm over head and, keeping it straight, gently stretch, reaching away from the body. Hold each stretch for six seconds

1.3 Explaining two approaches to develop performance.

2.3 Selecting and applying two approaches to impact positively on a performance.

These methods are valid approaches you could explain and use to develop flexibility to achieve these standards.

Principles of training summary: flexibility

Frequency	Intensity	Duration	Progressive overload	Specificity
Every day.	Until you feel a gentle stretch.	10–15 minutes, with each stretch held for 5–10 seconds.	Stretch a little further, hold, stretch for longer or add in more stretches.	Stretch the muscles most needed in the activity you are preparing for.

Monitoring and evaluating

By recording your flexibility training via a training diary (see page 213 for example) you will be able to keep an accurate record of the stretches you did, how you felt and also what you planned to do next.

2.4 Monitoring and recording performance development sessions.

These methods are good ways to have an accurate, reliable record of what you actually did each session. Providing evidence of the use of these methods would help you achieve the assessment standard.

Whatever methods you use to gather information on your performance will include getting feedback from others. Indeed, you might on occasion be the person giving feedback to a partner who has just finished a sequence. This feedback might be in the form of completing an observation schedule or being the assistant measuring one of the standardised tests. At all times this means you must be willing to take on board feedback given and to use it to help develop your performance further.

✔ Assessment in PE

3.1 Seeking feedback from others.

The record of what you did to test the progress you made when developing this aspect of fitness includes feedback, which you will be able to use to achieve this assessment standard.

By repeating the tests you should be able to see improvements in your scores, indicating that your flexibility has improved – as long as you have conducted the second tests under the same conditions as the first test. For example, if you conducted the first test in a warm gym and the second test outside on a cold rainy day, it is possible that you would not see the improvements you might expect because of the weather and temperature of the surroundings.

Again, it is vital that you look for changes in your whole performance as a result of this improved flexibility. Can you lift your leg up higher when dancing? Is your pike position in trampolining more effective? Is your tennis service more effective because of increased flexibility in your shoulder joint?

✔ Assessment in PE

3.2 Evaluating the effectiveness of the personal development plan in supporting performance development.

3.3 Evaluating progress based on all information gathered.

It is valuable to look at your overall performance when trying to prove that your development programme has been effective. The approaches you used to develop your performance should also be the focus of this evaluation process. This will help you identify if the type of stretching you have used has been appropriate and any progress made in improving flexibility will be able to be measured. This will help you prove the effectiveness of your personal development plan.

Future needs

Flexibility is an area of performance that requires ongoing attention. By building a series of stretches into your training and preparation for performance you will be able to keep flexibility improving and prevent injury.

Unfortunately age sometimes means injuries happen more often. With care and attention to flexibility this can be reduced.

Check your progress

Complete the following to check your understanding	HELP NEEDED	GETTING THERE	CONFIDENT
1. Explain what you understand about flexibility.	◯	◯	◯
2. Describe how you would gather information about your flexibility.	◯	◯	◯
3. Explain how the muscles work to move a joint.	◯	◯	◯
4. Describe a programme of work you could carry out to develop your flexibility.	◯	◯	◯
5. Explain how would you evaluate the success of your programme of work.	◯	◯	◯

Make a judgement – were you able to complete these easily? If not, go back and look over some of the explanations or speak to your teacher for further advice.

Feature of the factor: local muscular endurance (LME)

Local muscular endurance can be described as the ability of groups of muscles to work together continuously during exercise.

GO! Activity

Set up a 'pentathlon' containing some of the following activities:

Constant rally against the wall for three minutes.

Cycling constantly for three minutes.

Blocking constantly ten times in a row.

Lay up ten times in a row.

Jump to defend a rebound ten times.

As you complete each 'station' tick the chart to identify which muscle groups are being used repeatedly.

Having completed the stations you will be able to experience the feeling of the muscles working continuously without rest for a period of time. Use the diagram on page 70 to identify which muscle groups are being used repeatedly.

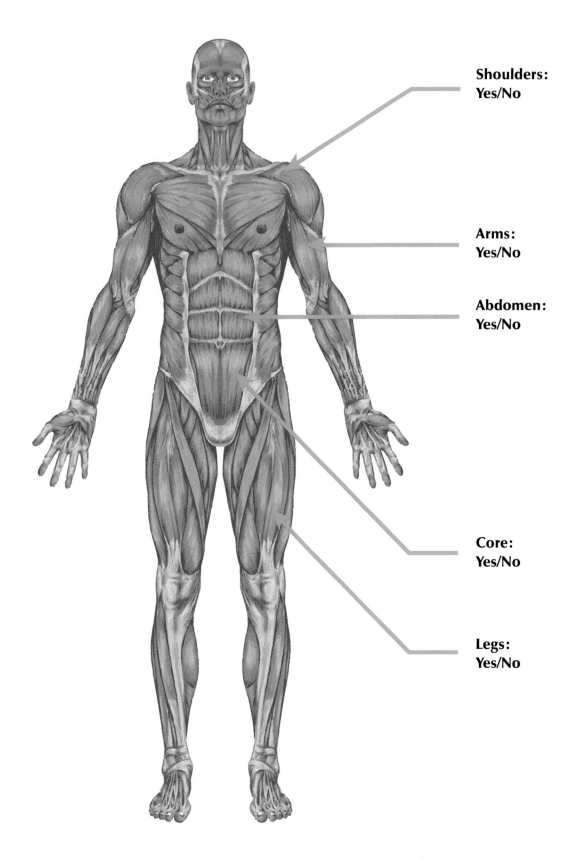

Shoulders:
Yes/No

Arms:
Yes/No

Abdomen:
Yes/No

Core:
Yes/No

Legs:
Yes/No

This diagram can be downloaded from the Leckie and Leckie website at www.leckieandleckie.co.uk/n45physicaled

GO! Activity

This can be a class task, individual task or a homework exercise. Describe how the different muscle groups felt as you worked through the tasks. Make a spider diagram of words that gives some detail about what different people felt as they went round the stations.

Here is an example:

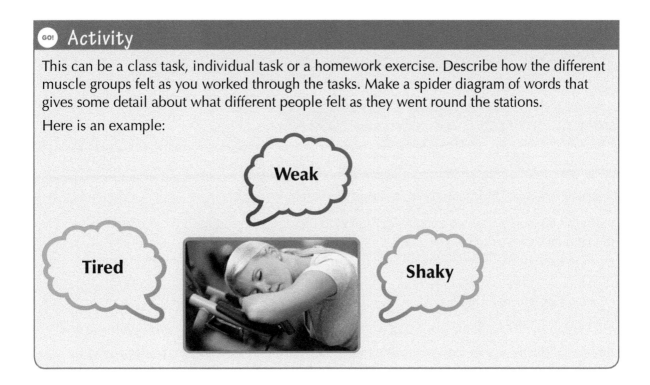

How does LME impact positively on performance?

Good LME in physical activity allows the performer to keep a high standard of skill throughout an activity. For example, a trampolinist would be able to keep a good shape, with toes pointed and arms extended at every bounce throughout her whole sequence. This would mean she would score more points. A footballer with good levels of LME in his legs would be able to consistently tackle and win the ball and keep possession from the opposition all the way to the end of the match.

How does lack of LME impact negatively on performance?

With poor levels of LME a performer can lose quality in their movements as the activity goes on. This means they might lose accuracy when returning the shuttle or no longer be able to keep jumping to spike the ball when given a good set in volleyball. This is a waste and means the opposition does not need to set the block against the attack. This would mean the opposition can conserve their energy, making it easy for them to build their own attack out of weak and poor returns.

ⓖⓞ! Activity

Make another table of all the skills involved in one activity.

Here is an example.

Activity: football	Muscle group used
Passing	Legs and core
Running	Legs
Tackling	Legs, arms, shoulders and core

From the table of your own activity identify the main muscles required for overall effective performance in your activity.

☑ Assessment in PE

1.2 Explaining in detail the impact of one positive and one negative factor on performance.

By being able to explain how you felt when taking part in this activity you will be able to explain the positive or negative impact LME could have on your performance.

How do I gather information on LME?

In order to begin to understand how levels of LME affect performance, it is necessary to gather information about the whole performance. This allows us to begin to get data about the areas of performance that need attention.

By looking at the timing in a dance performance when a jump is completed it should be clear to see if the height of the jump decreases as the dance goes on. This would indicate poor LME.

In hockey, a player's lack of LME might show itself by a midfielder being unable to pass the ball accurately when she is tiring. Her poor LME means her arms and shoulders are too tired to be able to keep doing the correct technique to pass the ball out of danger.

A general observation schedule might look like this:

Insert a tick or cross	0–5 mins	5–10 mins	10–15 mins	15–20 mins	20–25 mins	25–30 mins	30–35 mins
Passing accurate							
Tackling effective							
Dodging effective							
Shooting effective							

You should modify this to include the skills (e.g. passing, hitting, tackling) you want to observe in your performance, and arrange to film your performance if possible, to ensure your observations are accurate and reliable.

Collecting information about the success of skills that need to be repeated throughout a performance is a good measurement of LME.

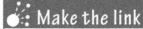

✔ Assessment in PE

1.1 Explaining in detail two methods used to identify factors impacting on performance.

By using knowledge about the methods used to collect data on LME you will be able to achieve this standard. You must provide a clear explanation of how these methods were organised and put into practice.

Make the link

You have used general observation schedules (GOS) and POOCH analysis sheets in other areas of your course to identify **P**roblems, **O**ptions, **O**utcomes and **Ch**oices, allowing you to think and reflect on what is happening in a performance (problems) and to identify possible solutions (options and outcomes) from a range of different options (choices). These provide accurate data on LME too.

You might also set up some tests to measure the LME capabilities of sets of muscles. For example, count how many sit-ups, step-ups, press-ups and tricep dips you can do in one minute.

You could use the table below to help you record the number of each exercise you complete in a minute.

Muscle group	Method to identify the impact	Number of repetitions completed in a minute
Legs	Step-ups	
Abdominals	Sit-ups	
Shoulders	Press-ups	
Arms	Tricep dips	

Appropriateness of data collection

By looking at the skills you use repeatedly in an activity and evaluating how effective they are throughout the whole performance you will have gathered very useful information. Then, by measuring the number of repetitions you can complete of each exercise, you will be able to go back and repeat the test after training to get a clear indication of whether your training programme has improved your LME.

When you are confident that LME is a feature you see as a training priority then a programme of work can be organised. The principles of training must be used in order that training can have the desired effect.

Preparation for performance development

When planning a programme of work to improve our LME the same 'rules' or principles apply as those we have used when working on all other aspects of fitness. Remember we used the acronym SPORT.

S is for **specific**
P is for **progression**
O is for **overload**
R is for **reversibility**
T is for **tedium**

These are the **principles of training**.

By using these principles we:

- Plan **what** we do in our training to develop our LME.
- **Develop the training** as we go along.
- Make sure the training is interesting and worthwhile, thereby positively impacting on our performance.

With LME training we again need to gradually make the demands of our training programme more challenging by working harder (**intensity**), working for longer (**duration**) or working for more sessions each week (**frequency**). This is called **progressive overload**. We also need to make sure we consider any changes we need to make to our training if for any reason we stop. We lose fitness quickly (**reversibility**) and must reduce the training we do when we return after injury or absence. By keeping training interesting we prevent boredom and low levels of motivation while training (**tedium**).

The LME training you do must be **specific** to the activity you are focusing on, the role you have in that activity and the muscle groups you use most often. This means your training will be directed at making your LME better for your chosen activity.

By applying these principles to the training you plan to do the more likely it is that you will be successful in improving your LME.

☑ Assessment in PE

2.2 Preparing and implementing a personal development plan containing clearly identified development targets.

The principles of training should be used when you put together your development plan and as you work through your plan they must be applied to make sure your progress is steady.

Approaches to develop performance

Circuit training is one popular approach to improve LME. The stations can be set up in a way to ensure the skills and activities used in the circuit develop the muscle groups required most in the performer's activity. Traditionally things like step-ups, sit-ups and burpees have been used to form part of a circuit training programme as they isolate the muscles used for skills such as running, passing, tackling and jumping. Today, light weights are often included and very specific activity-related movements can be included to make sure the training has the maximum impact. In netball, for example, squads of players can be seen working through dodging drills to build up LME in the lower leg to allow constant changes of direction.

Within a circuit there are a number of ways progress can be monitored. A coach might organise for everyone to complete the circuit as quickly as possible and then record their finishing times. Or each performer might do each station for one minute, counting how many repetitions they do at every station. This is recorded as a performer's maximum, and the training load they would use each training session would be half of this maximum. This would be gradually increased to make sure the performer keeps improving. This is the same principle used to develop CRE.

The performer should feel the signs when it is time to overload the circuit training session. For example, they should finish the sets of the circuit quicker and should feel that the muscle groups they are working can do the repetitions much more easily without tiring. These things are clear signs that LME is improving.

The data generated on the record card can be used to add more repetitions, more stations or even more sets to the circuit training session.

GO! Activity

With some support you should be able to create a station for an LME circuit.

Experiment with ideas for actions you can repeat over and over again. Could you do these actions holding a light hand weight? Once you have agreed what your station is to be, draw it out with instructions on flip chart paper. This should include details of the equipment you need, the area where you will do this and exactly what it is that is to be repeated. Here is an example:

Activity: trampolining

Area of focus requiring LME: arms swinging up above head with every bounce.

Circuit station: double arm lift with 2 kg weights.

Instructions: keeping shoulders down, repeatedly lift the weight above head until the arms are straight. Repeat ten times (one set) then move to the next station. Come back and do two more sets as part of the overall circuit training session.

The group should now split into two. One half stays at their station while the others move round trying the range of stations organised by the class. The group that remains at the station is responsible for explaining the purpose of their proposed plan to the visitors moving around the circuit. The groups then swap and fulfil the other role.

Further developing LME

Here is an example of a circuit for a netball player who wants to develop LME in their arms and legs so that they can be more effective.

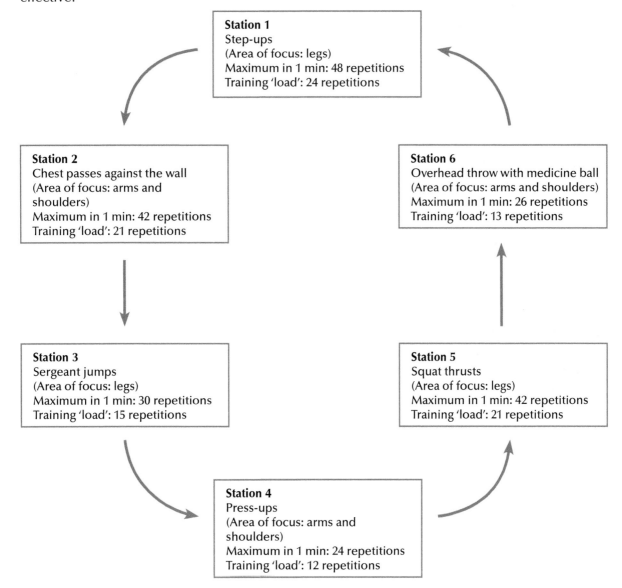

Station 1
Step-ups
(Area of focus: legs)
Maximum in 1 min: 48 repetitions
Training 'load': 24 repetitions

Station 2
Chest passes against the wall
(Area of focus: arms and shoulders)
Maximum in 1 min: 42 repetitions
Training 'load': 21 repetitions

Station 3
Sergeant jumps
(Area of focus: legs)
Maximum in 1 min: 30 repetitions
Training 'load': 15 repetitions

Station 4
Press-ups
(Area of focus: arms and shoulders)
Maximum in 1 min: 24 repetitions
Training 'load': 12 repetitions

Station 5
Squat thrusts
(Area of focus: legs)
Maximum in 1 min: 42 repetitions
Training 'load': 21 repetitions

Station 6
Overhead throw with medicine ball
(Area of focus: arms and shoulders)
Maximum in 1 min: 26 repetitions
Training 'load': 13 repetitions

Doing all six stations once would be **one set**. Training starts with **three sets** of the training loads. Record the time taken to complete all three sets on your circuit training card.

Next, decide which of the stations fit well together and could combine to make a personalised circuit for each member of the class. Decisions have to be made about which of the stations fit your own personal development needs.

From here a record has to be made of which stations you are using, how many repetitions and sets of each you are going to do and how many times a week you will do them.

⟡ CfE focus

Taking responsibility for investigating, creating and implementing a personalised circuit station is a worthwhile activity. It makes you think for yourself, encourages you to explain and justify your views and make decisions based on knowledge and experience. These are all features of being a **responsible citizen**.

Principles of training summary: LME

Frequency	Intensity	Duration	Progressive overload	Specificity
Three times a week.	50% of maximum completed in a minute.	Timed sessions or completing sets in as quick a time as possible.	Add more stations, increase repetitions, number of sets or reduce rests between sets.	Use stations with muscle groups that are required for the focus activity.

Monitoring and evaluating

⁘ Make the link

Using circuit training as an approach of training uses the same process and principles you applied when working on your CRE.

GO! Activity

Design a circuit training card to keep a record of the number of repetitions, sets and stations you complete during each session. Each time you do this training complete the card and save as a permanent record of the work you did and the progress you made using this method of training. This allows you to monitor the progress you are making and to ensure that session-to-session and week-to-week you are increasing the amount of work you do to make sure your performance continually improves. See Chapter 8 for an example of monitoring a circuit training session.

✎ Fact

Circuit comes from the Latin word *circuitus*, which means 'to go around'.

As you work within a group you will be able to get feedback from your teacher about the time taken to complete the circuit. Also, the feedback you get when re-doing your GOS and/or your standardised tests will tell you if the training you completed was worthwhile. If your LME has improved then it would be fair to say that we would expect to see improvements in your overall performance. This would be a good indication of whether your programme of work has been successful or not.

☑ Assessment in PE

3.1 Seeking feedback from others.

3.2 Evaluating the effectiveness of the personal development plan in supporting performance development.

3.3 Evaluating progress based on all information gathered.
By reflecting on the results you collect after retesting you should be able to **evaluate** the progress you have made in improving your LME. If you are able to keep your arm action in the 200 m front crawl race more consistent as the race progresses, or are able to keep a smooth, fluent bounce height in your trampolining sequence, then it is likely you have been able to make improvements in your LME in your leg muscles.

Future needs

Your future needs in terms of LME might be to continue to focus on this area to ensure your ability to repeat a skill over and over again. However, you might also decide that a different area requires your attention.

☑ Assessment in PE

3.4 Identifying and explaining future development needs.

By making accurate judgements about your new levels of LME you are able to look at your whole performance again and try to identify what area you might want to focus on next. It could be that LME will remain an area you still want to work on or it could be, for example, that core strength improvement is an area you feel needs attention because of the posture requirements of your chosen activity.

Check your progress

Complete the following to check your understanding.

	HELP NEEDED	GETTING THERE	CONFIDENT
1. Explain how local muscular endurance can impact on your performance.	◯	◯	◯
2. Describe one method to gather information on your LME.	◯	◯	◯
3. Describe one station of a circuit training programme you used to develop your LME.	◯	◯	◯
4. Explain how you would overload your training to develop your LME.	◯	◯	◯
5. Describe what performance would look like with improved LME.	◯	◯	◯

Make a judgement – were you able to complete these easily? If not, go back and look over some of the explanations or speak to your teacher for further advice.

2 The physical factor: aspects of skill fitness

This chapter deals with all the skill fitness features that have an impact on performance.

The features we are learning to identify and develop are:

- Agility
- Coordination
- Reaction time

In this chapter you will learn:

1. How agility, coordination and reaction time can impact on performance.
2. How to gather information about these features.
3. How to prepare for performance development.
4. To understand and apply approaches to develop performance.
5. To monitor performance development.
6. To evaluate performance development.
7. To identify and explain future performance development needs.

🧠 What should I already know?

As part of the activities you learned in your BGE you will have explored the aspect of skill-related fitness. Perhaps during games you will have looked at how these aspects contribute to make your performance more effective. (HWB 4-22a) or examined the contribution they would make when taking part in creative activities.

Feature of the factor: agility

Agility is required for almost every performer in every activity. The ability to start and stop quickly and to change direction while staying in control is essential. Agility is a combination of speed and flexibility, and when used effectively in a performance situation can give you fluency and control. Agile performers can make an activity look effortless and easy. Agile performers are able to move around the floor, pitch, court or pool with ease, conserving their energy, combining minimum effort with maximum efficiency.

How does agility impact positively on performance?

Good agility in a games situation can allow a player to change direction quickly, 'wrongfooting' an opponent. This gives a tremendous advantage and can lead to defenders making rash tackles when trying to win back possession. We all know of footballers who are recognised as being great 'tricksters' and are difficult to dispossess.

Being able to change your body position quickly is an asset in badminton too. An opponent will find it difficult to out-manoeuvre you if you are agile. You can move easily from sideline to sideline and from back to front court quickly if you are agile – eventually leading to frustration on the opponent's part and to you being able to take control of the match.

GO! Activity

Use the internet to research some of the great players who have demonstrated effective agility when performing.

Look at a range of activities from team sports to martial arts and creative activities.

Here are some examples of athletes to investigate:

- Cristiano Ronaldo (football, Real Madrid)
- Lionel Messi (football, Barcelona)
- Tamika Catchings (USA women's basketball)
- Daniel Purvis (gymnastics)
- Andy Murray (tennis)

Are you able to identify examples of how these athletes use agility to be effective performers?

Brainstorm the words you would use to describe these athletes' ability. Display the words on a flip chart poster.

How does lack of agility impact negatively on performance?

In contrast, lack of agility makes us easy targets in most games. In volleyball, poor agility leads to the opposition targeting a player who is slow to get into position to return the spike. The spiker, when choosing where to place his attacking shot, would look to play the ball outwith the range of a player who had demonstrated they were unable to change direction quickly. This would mean a team would have a weakness, which they would have to try to address.

In dance, agility allows the performer to make the choreography look interesting. If a dancer is unable to move quickly around the stage in different directions, changing levels and using a variety of tempos, then the overall performance lacks excitement and is uninteresting.

☑ Assessment in PE

1.2 Explaining in detail the impact of one positive and one negative factor on performance.

This section helps you to understand how agility can impact on any activity. By looking carefully at the demands of your activity you should be able to explain how skill-related aspects of fitness can make your performance more effective.

2.1 Describing strengths and areas for development in a performance.

By applying this knowledge to your own performance you can work out if agility is an area you need to develop.

◇ CfE focus

By looking at the range of environments where agility is useful you are demonstrating ability to 'apply critical thinking.' This is a useful skill in many situations where you may have to make decisions about what is the best course of action. This means you are an **effective contributor**.

Skills for life, learning and work

Presentation skills – by presenting your findings about the effectiveness of an athlete's use of agility you are taking on a leadership role. This will be useful if you go on to study further after school or in the workplace when you might need to put together a presentation for other staff. This is an employability skill.

How do I gather information on agility?

In every performance development situation the first point is always to identify what the whole performance looks like and how agility impacts on it positively or negatively. The method you might use is a general observation schedule. You will need to look at all aspects involved in the activity to try to assess if agility affects the kind of things you need to do within the performance. Criteria like dodging past opponents in football or getting your feet in position quickly for the push-off at the tumble turn are things you might want to look at. For example, the criteria might be:

Activity: hockey

Criteria from model performer	Satisfactory	Needs improvement
Passing		
Dribbling		
Shooting		
Tackling		
Dodging		
Slapping		
Flicking		

From there it would be vital to get more focused and factual information about your agility. There are a number of standardised tests available to measure agility. The best-known and most straightforward one to use is the Illinois agility test.

Fact

Dan 'dirty' Kerr of Australia holds the world record for the Illinois agility test. His time of 11.4 seconds, achieved in July 2007, has never been broken.

GO! Activity

Follow the link above to access the protocol for the Illinois agility test and the averages you can compare your results to.

Set up and complete the test.

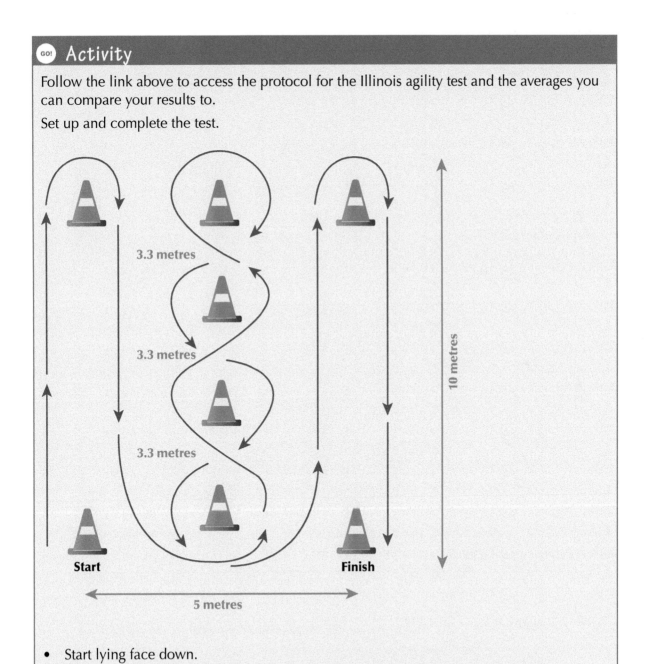

- Start lying face down.
- When the whistle blows, get up and sprint around the course as fast as possible.
- When finished the performer is told the time it took to cover the course.

GO! Activity

Another test that can be used is the T test for agility.

It is set up as follows:

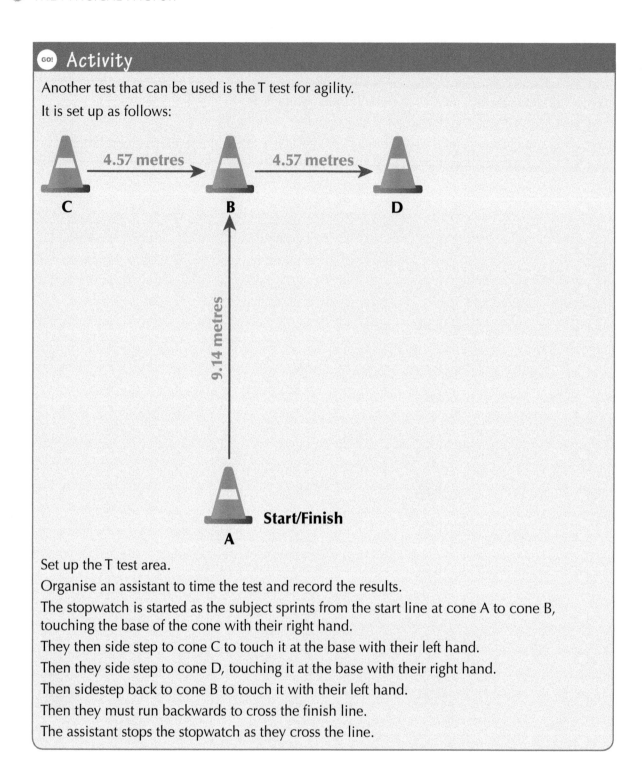

Set up the T test area.

Organise an assistant to time the test and record the results.

The stopwatch is started as the subject sprints from the start line at cone A to cone B, touching the base of the cone with their right hand.

They then side step to cone C to touch it at the base with their left hand.

Then they side step to cone D, touching it at the base with their right hand.

Then sidestep back to cone B to touch it with their left hand.

Then they must run backwards to cross the finish line.

The assistant stops the stopwatch as they cross the line.

Appropriateness of the methods of data collection

By looking first at our whole performance we are able to see how agility affects us. This means when we have completed some training to try to improve agility we can go back and look again to compare and see if overall performance has improved. There would be little point in improving agility if it didn't actually have a positive impact on overall performance.

 Assessment in PE

In the portfolio you will be able to write about the planning you undertook when getting ready to begin developing performance.

Preparation for performance development

For agility, it is important that the type of training you do matches the types of movements used in your activity. Therefore training is **specific** to the demands of the activity. For example, agility training for badminton is different from the agility training a basketball player would do. This is because of the different types of movements used in each activity.

 Activity

After participating in your chosen activity complete the following POOCH analysis.

STAGES OF POOCH		Your response
PROBLEM	What problem does poor agility give you in this activity?	
OPTIONS	Brainstorm any possible solutions based on what you know already about agility.	
OUTCOMES	What are the pros and cons of the possible solutions you have come up with?	
CHOICE	Make a decision about the option you have chosen to follow.	
HOW SUCCESSFUL?	What worked or was useful? Can we build on the success gained here or do we need to go back and look at the problem again?	

 Make the link

This process of examining the impact of agility on your performance asks you to reflect on what you already know in order that you can 'refine' your training ideas to plan a programme of work to impact positively on your performance. This encourages you to take 'measured risks' and examine/experiment with alternatives as you try to develop your agility.

Approaches that impact positively on performance

Agility circuits are generally fun and allow the performer to work on activity-related skills to help develop quickness and whole body movement. These circuits need to 'mimic' the kinds of movements involved in the activity if they are to be of any use. For example, a netball player would work on quick chasse movements as she moved round the edge of the circle. This would allow her to isolate and rehearse/practise and develop the movements in a less competitive situation. In time, if the movements are practised while concentrating on matching the exact way they are repeated in a game, then improvements in the whole game will be observed.

An agility circuit for a hockey player might look like this:

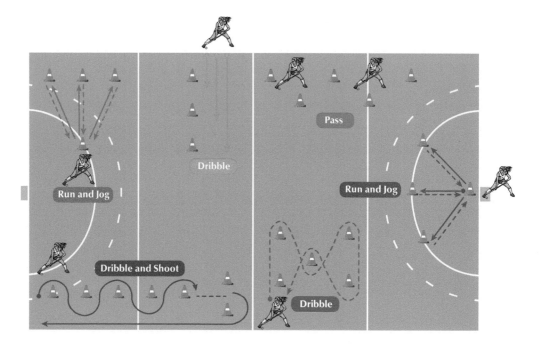

GO! Activity

Design an agility drill for one aspect of performance that requires agility.

Watch as the rest of the class demonstrate the drills they have created. Choose five of the drills to combine with your own to become your agility training circuit. Set the circuit up and complete one set with a two-minute rest period between each station.

By using this circuit three times a week, agility should improve. Keep a note of how long it takes you to complete the six stations. As you improve, this time should decrease. To progressively overload the circuit, you could add in another station, decrease the rest periods between each station or try to decrease the time it takes you to complete the whole circuit.

Principles of training: agility

Frequency	Intensity	Duration	Progressive overload	Specificity
Three times a week.	At high pace using the following: week 1, 50% of max; weeks 3 and 4, 55% of max; weeks 5 and 6, 60% of max.	10–15 minutes.	Add in another station, do each station faster, make the sessions longer or cut rest periods.	Use drills that are similar to the types of movements required in the focus activity.

✔ Assessment in PE

2.2 Preparing and implementing a personal development plan containing clearly identified development targets.

By using this method you will be able to demonstrate how agility can be developed. You will need to demonstrate how each station will be carried out and how you would change/progress the plan as the sessions continued.

Monitoring and evaluating

Keep a note of the training you are completing. You can do this by using a training diary to record how long it takes you to complete each session, how you feel and what your plans are for increasing or overloading the training. You can also film the training you do, making sure you also record the time it takes you to complete the circuit and that the quality of your movements remains high.

You will need to use an assistant to tell you when to start your training, when to rest between stations and what your finishing time is. This feedback needs to be written down or stored somewhere to make sure you are always making progress as you train.

As you train and keep a close eye on the progress you are making you will be able to make judgements about the effectiveness of the training you complete. It would be wise to complete another POOCH analysis to identify within your overall performance if agility has improved. Or you could re-do your general observation schedule and compare before and after results to assess the impact of agility after training.

✔ Assessment in PE

3.2 Evaluating the effectiveness of the personal development plan in supporting performance development.

3.3 Evaluating progress based on all information gathered.

By duplicating the original methods and comparing the before and after training results you can identify improvements. You can then write up a before and after profile of your performance, which will allow you to plan which areas you should focus on next.

Future needs

By retesting and evaluating the process you have completed you will be able to identify any areas relating to agility that still require focus. By then attempting to modify what you did to further improve your performance, future needs can be addressed. Future needs often relate to continuing the training you were doing but in a reduced capacity. This will keep your agility 'ticking over' while you go on to focus on a new development need. For example, footballers often complete a variety of drills aimed at keeping their agility at a high level for the whole season.

✔ Assessment in PE

3.4 Identifying and explaining future needs.

By using an example from your overall performance to show how your agility still needs attention you will be able to explain why you decided to keep focusing on this aspect of fitness.

Check your progress

Complete the following to check your understanding.

	HELP NEEDED	GETTING THERE	CONFIDENT
1. Describe how you would set up the Illinois agility test.	◯	◯	◯
2. Explain how agility can be used to improve performance.	◯	◯	◯
3. Describe a drill you could include as part of an agility circuit.	◯	◯	◯
4. Explain how you would develop your training.	◯	◯	◯
5. Describe a method used to monitor the training you were carrying out.	◯	◯	◯

Make a judgement – were you able to complete these easily? If not, go back and look over some of the explanations or speak to your teacher for further advice.

Feature of the factor: coordination

Coordination is the ability of two or more parts of the body to work together to produce a movement. A person who is said to be 'coordinated' makes movements look easy, effortless and fluent. They generally have success with these movements. That means when making a pass to someone in their team, the ball generally goes where they want it to go. A trampolinist demonstrates coordination when her arms and legs move in perfect synchronisation as she twists to complete swivel hips. Coordination allows minimum effort with maximum effect. That means energy is not wasted and the outcome of the movement (the pass or the swivel hips) is usually interesting to watch – it is **aesthetically pleasing**.

GO! Activity

Make a list of the activities your class finds aesthetically pleasing.

Try to then explain what it is that makes the performance interesting to watch.

For example when watching Jessica Ennis compete in the Heptathlon Hurdles event, the strength and power she showed as she ran a personal best in the Hurdles competition was interesting to watch. She had to run powerfully down the track to get as much speed as possible and at the same time coordinate her jumps to perfection so as not to break stride. It all just fitted together perfectly and looked almost effortless.

Coordination and the senses

Interestingly, although coordination involves two or more parts of your body moving together, your senses are involved to a high degree too. Your senses – in particular **sight, hearing** and **kinaesthetic** all contribute to helping your body parts move at the right time, with the right amount of force, speed and control.

Sight

This involves your brain trying to take in all it sees as important in a performance situation. For example:

- Where is the person I want to pass the ball to?
- How far away are they?
- Are there any obstacles in the way?

Hearing

The sound of someone shouting for a pass might guide you towards passing in a particular direction. However, the sound of a defender approaching to tackle might also make you pass in a different direction.

Kinaesthetic

This is how you feel as you perform. When performing, our kinaesthetic senses give us feedback about what the **movements feel like** as we do them.

As you shoot in football the **way your foot contacts** the ball instantly tells you if you have done it correctly. By then **seeing** where the ball goes and **hearing** the sound the perfect kick makes as it leaves the foot, the body is using kinaesthetic feedback to judge if the shot will be successful.

In basketball when shooting you would **feel** if you had got all the parts of the skill right **as** the ball left your hand. Then, if the ball goes into the hoop, your **sight** confirms these feelings by seeing the points scored.

⚫ Make the link

You will have looked at catching, throwing and jumping in many of the activities you have covered in your broad general education. You will remember that you need to look where the ball or shuttle is coming from when trying to catch or hit.

⚫ Make the link

In the skills section of this book you will learn about skilled and model performers. A performer who is said to be coordinated is likely to be at the automatic stage of learning, where they **do not have to think** about how to **do** the skill.

🔵 Activity

Identify within your class skills the group feel they can do without thinking about them. For example:

- A golf drive
- An overhead clear
- A reverse stick stop in indoor hockey
- A backward roll into a handstand
- A backdrop in trampolining
- A top spin serve in table tennis
- A spike in volleyball

Your teacher will set up for you to try some of these skills while you try to focus on what your senses tell you as you carry out the skill.

(continued)

For example:

'In the backdrop in trampolining because I **see** the ceiling as I go back I am able to watch that I go straight back, staying near the middle of the bed. Also, as I contact the bed, I can **feel** if I land on exactly the middle of my back, not too high on my shoulders, which might make me begin to rotate over my head into a back somersault, and not too low on my back, which means I will find it difficult to get back to my feet.'

'When using my reverse stick stop in hockey I can **feel** if my hands are in the correct position as my feet move and I bend my knees to get low to the ground. As I trap the ball I can **see** my stick and body are in the correct positions. Even the **sound** the trapping of the ball makes give me confidence that I have performed the skill correctly.'

As well as using your senses, coordination means using your body parts in the correct order and at the correct time. Effectively you are using, all your senses to create a positive outcome. This means linking together arm actions, leg actions, striking actions, jumping, changes of direction and many other combinations of body parts.

⊙ Activity

For the skills you used in the previous activity, can you identify the different parts of the body that were involved in producing the movements?

Make an inventory of the different body parts used for one skill to be completed effectively.

An inventory is a list of all the parts required to make the skill happen.

For example:

Coordination inventory: badminton overhead clear

Body part/senses	Coordination required
Head	Looking at shuttle, slightly tilted up
Legs	Feet apart, weight on back foot
Arms	Non-racquet arm 'sighting' the shuttle, racquet arm behind head, shoulder dropped
Body	Turned side on, ready to twist round quickly to add to the transfer of weight
Sight	Watch for shuttle, focus on hitting it in front of and above head
Hearing	Listen for sound of clean hit in the centre of the racquet head and the noise of the fast throwing action of the racquet being brought through quickly

How does coordination impact positively on performance?

In many activities, coordination is the defining aspect of performance that will determine success or failure.

By being able to pass the ball where it needs to go, your team will hopefully stay in possession and so have more opportunities to score goals and win.

In cricket, a bowler with good coordination can run forward to the wicket and at the right time throw the ball with pace and direction towards the stumps while still being in control of his whole body. He uses his senses to see where the space is near the wicket and feels the rhythm of his run up and the release of the ball. In a fielding role, he can also move quickly to reach and catch a ball while at full stretch, landing without dropping it.

Another example of good coordination in swimming is when using the front crawl. The combination of the arm pull, leg action and breathing pattern produce a coordinated, efficient stroke. This means the swimmer can go faster through the water and achieve the fastest time possible. She is able to **feel** the pattern of the arms and legs working together with her breathing to make one smooth movement sequence.

In creative activities good coordination enables a performer to be able to make skills look good – aesthetically pleasing – and to link together skills in a way which allows the sequence of movements to flow. A skilled dancer is able to **feel** if the dance fits together smoothly.

How does lack of coordination impact negatively on performance?

Lack of coordination is easy to identify. Any throwing action that lacks coordination looks clumsy and results in the ball being intercepted or not going to the intended target.

A volleyball player with poor coordination will not be able to get his arms into the correct position at the same time as bending his legs to get low enough to play a good dig towards his setter. This would result in the setter having to move to try to get to this poor first pass and would possibly mean that his team's attack would be less effective.

When tackling in hockey, poor coordination might mean you would contact your opponent's stick instead of the ball. This would result in a free hit against you.

Gymnasts with poor coordination find it challenging to change direction with ease, to add in turns and twists to make sequences more interesting and demanding. This means the ordinary, straightforward combination of skills achieves fewer points. Lack of coordination might also mean that legs are not held together during balances or arms are not symmetrical as a handspring is completed.

☑ Assessment in PE

2.1 Describing strengths and areas for development in a performance.

Information gathered about the success of your passing in a game, the points lost in a gymnastics sequence for poor coordination, the number of times you miss the shuttle in badminton, will indicate whether coordination is a problem. To achieve this assessment standard you would need to give details about what parts of your performance are affected by your lack of coordination.

How do I gather information on coordination?

In a whole performance, coordination can be measured against criteria such as: lands with two feet, arms straight. In a game situation, having identified through a general observation schedule that there is a problem with accuracy of the skills of passing, tackling or catching, a more focused data analysis would be needed. This would break down the skill into its three component parts: Preperation, Action and Recovery.

From here there are standardised tests that can be used to get an objective measurement of coordination. One of these is a simple Alternate Hand Wall Throwing test. This could be adapted to measure kicking or striking. The aim of the test is to throw the ball off the wall with one hand then catch with the other hand. This test might be useful for a performer who has to throw and catch a lot during their activity.

📌 fact

David Slick from the USA holds the Guinness World Record for juggling three objects for the longest duration. He juggled continuously for 12 hours and 13 minutes – an amazingly lengthy display of hand – eye coordination.

Make the link

In the Skills section of this book there is more detailed information on how skills are broken down into preparation, action and recovery stages.

GO! Activity

Begin this hand–eye coordination test by drawing a line two metres from the wall, where the subject will stand. The subject throws the ball with his right hand and catches with his left. He does this for 30 seconds. The recorder keeps a record of the total number of passes caught and thrown in the 30 seconds. As with all of these tests there are norms or average rating, which you can use to identify if your hand–eye coordination is poor, average, good or excellent.

	Excellent	Above average	Average	Below average	Poor
Age 15–16	> 35 passes	30–35 passes	25–29 passes	20–24 passes	<20 passes

Another test used to measure coordination is the plate tapping test. In this test the subject has to touch two discs alternately laid out on a table in front of them. The discs have to be touched 50 times, as quickly as possible. The discs should be 20 cm in diameter. The other hand is placed on a rectangle marked out on the table, which is equidistant from both discs. This rectangle should be 30 cm long and 20 cm wide. The time taken to complete this task is recorded.

Age group	Extemely below average	Below average	Average	Above average	Extremely above average
Girls aged 13	>14.5 secs	13.2–14.5	11.8–13.1	10.4–11.7	<10.4
Boys aged 13	>15.1	13.5–15.1	11.8–13.4	10.2–11.7	<10.2
Girls aged 14	>14.1	12.2–13.4	10.8–12.1	9.5–10.7	<9.5
Boys aged 14	>14.1	12.4–14.1	10.6–12.3	8.8–10.5	<8.8
Girls aged 15–18	>12.1	11.9–12.1	10.5–11.8	9.3–10.4	<9.3
Boys aged 15–18	>13.2	11.7–13.2	10.2–11.6	8.6–10.1	<8.6

For a hockey, badminton or volleyball player perhaps these tests are not really relevant.

An alternative coordination test for these team activities might be passing to a target while on the move (see GO! Activity below).

GO! Activity

Design your own coordination test for hockey, badminton or volleyball.

Step 1 Identify a skill from the activity that requires coordination.

Step 2 Decide what equipment you need to carry out the test.

Step 3 Check with your teacher that the test is valid and reliable.

Step 4 Carry out the test.

Example: The spike in volleyball

Step 1

Chalk is needed to mark a 1-metre by 1-metre box on the floor at the right- and left-hand sideline of the volleyball court. Three volleyballs, one feeder and one retriever of the ball are needed, as well as a recorder to note my results.

Step 2

The feeder hand feeds the ball for me to run in and jump to spike from the same place ten times, with a 30-second rest for recovery in between. The feed must go to the same place each time. I must run and jump to spike the ball to the square on the left then the square on the right.

Step 3

The feeder waits for me to be ready, then feeds the ball to the same place ten times in a row for me to spike to the target areas. I should take sufficient rest to make sure the test is not affected by me being tired. The recorder keeps a record of how many spikes hit the target area.

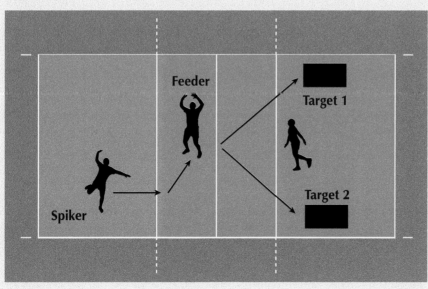

✔ Assessment in PE

1.1 Explaining in detail two methods used to identify factors impacting on performance.

These two methods could be explained to show how you set about testing your coordination.

Appropriateness of the methods of data collection

These methods of data collection are useful for gathering information about the coordination required for skills used as part of the activities in your course because they focus on skills used as part of that activity.

By making sure the test you use can be repeated, you are ensuring the results are reliable. By being clear about what the test involves and by keeping a note of results you are able to compare the two sets of results to check for improvements.

Preparation for performance development

Many opinions exist about how coordination can be developed. Some people think that beyond a certain age little can be done to improve a performer's coordination.

However, one thing most analysts agree on is that to develop coordination we need to reduce the speed at which the skill is practised. This is known as the Weber Fechner rule. The rule says that if we practise a skill requiring a great deal of coordination very slowly, then the brain begins to understand and remember the correct movement patterns required. Even when a skill is at the automatic stage of learning and the sub-routines of the movement are stored in our 'muscle memory', going through them again slowly can help and 'groove' the perfect technique.

Another theory used to help develop coordination is to take the skill out of the performance situation and practise it in isolation, with targets and time limits. Using this principle, the skill can be practised in a situation where the pressure is gradually increased. The skill is performed on its own, time after time, repeating the correct movement pattern quickly to specified targets.

The rule we need to remember at this stage is that we need to practise the **exact** technique over and over again to develop our coordination when using this skill. For example, a tennis player would work on their service for a long period of time to 'groove' the correct coordination required; a swimmer would isolate the arm action to focus on the correct hand position.

It is unlikely that you will do a programme of work solely to develop your coordination. However, understanding the need for coordination when performing skills is very important. Body parts and all of our senses must work together in a synchronised way to produce a successful outcome.

Make the link

This is very similar to some of the methods of practice you will come across in the Skills section of the book.

Approaches that impact positively on performance

The approaches we will look at that can be built into a performance development programme to improve coordination are activities that 'mimic' or copy the kinds of situations in which a skill would be performed. To this a target, time limit or special conditions are added. For example:

- **Multi-directional running:** chasse stepping quickly around the badminton court to improve court movement. This is very similar to drills you might use to develop agility. Giving a time limit and stating clearly that the player must turn side on when she gets to the corners of the court practises game-type movement under pressure and improves whole body coordination.

- **Mirroring drills with a partner:** mirroring the movement of a partner while dancing and reacting to changes of direction or changes of arm or leg movements when rehearsing a sequence.

Principles of training summary: coordination

Frequency	Intensity	Duration	Progressive overload	Specificity
As part of a training session for overall performance improvement.	As hard and fast as you can perform the drills.	10–15 minutes.	Add more targets, more demands to increase the difficulty of the drills.	Use drills that include movements/skills that are part of the focus activity.

Monitoring and evaluating

As with all performance development programmes, keeping an accurate record of work completed is essential. This could be done through using a training diary. Here, under a variety of headings, details should be recorded about how you felt during and after the training sessions, what you are going to focus on next and what progress you are making towards achieving the targets you have set yourself.

It is important to use feedback from your teacher and coaches about what improvements they have observed in your performance. You can use this information to reflect on whether your own kinaesthetic feedback is accurate. For example, if you feel your tumble turn has improved, does the teacher agree? If she does then it's likely that your skill has indeed developed. See Chapter 8 for an example of what a training diary might look like or where feedback could be recorded to help monitor your performance development.

✔ Assessment in PE

3.2 Evaluating the effectiveness of the personal development plan in supporting performance development.

3.3 Evaluating progress based on all information gathered.

To achieve these assessment standards you need to make evaluative judgments about how effective the practice is in improving your coordination. This means you can say clearly if it worked or not. You should also be able to identify changes in your whole performance to see if the training you did had any impact on the scores you achieved for your sequences, the final result in matches, or your times/distances achieved in athletics, for example.

Future needs

Coordination is an aspect of skill-related fitness that improves as you continue to use the developed skills in a performance situation.

That is, if you continue to use your coordination, you won't lose it!

In terms of future needs a realistic target would be to continue to keep possession of the ball, move your opponent around the court using a variety of strokes and to make sure your sequences in creative activities continue to be smooth, interesting, varied and linked together smoothly.

Check your progress

Complete the following to check your understanding.

	HELP NEEDED	GETTING THERE	CONFIDENT
1. Give two words that describe a coordinated performance.	⬭	⬭	⬭
2. Describe one human sense which helps make performance coordinated.	⬭	⬭	⬭
3. Give one example of the kind of information kinaesthetic awareness can give us when we perform a skill.	⬭	⬭	⬭
4. Describe in detail one test you used for coordination.	⬭	⬭	⬭
5. Explain one approach you used to develop coordination.	⬭	⬭	⬭
6. Describe how you evaluated any improvements in your overall performance after you had completed your programme of work.	⬭	⬭	⬭

Make a judgment – were you able to complete these easily? If not, go back and look over some of the explanations or speak to your teacher for further advice.

Feature of the factor: reaction time

Reaction time is an aspect of skill-related fitness within the physical factor area. It is your ability to respond quickly to what you see, hear or feel. In dance the first beat of the music might be the stimulus to make you begin your first motif. A guard would need to time their jump perfectly to get to the rebound before his opponent. In karate the defence of a high kick would need to be quick to prevent injury. A swimmer who can be first off the blocks and into the water is at a distinct advantage over her competitors.

In running the performer responds to the starter's gun – the stimulus. In netball the umpire's whistle is the stimulus for the players to sprint into the centre third to catch the centre pass, and in football the goalkeeper dives in reaction to the striker's shot at goal.

GO! Activity

Film an activity of your choice. Then watch the footage to try to identify any examples of where quick reaction times are required.

Examples you might capture are:

- A player reacting to a smash being played at her.
- A quick response to a top-spin serve in table tennis.

Reaction time is affected by a number of things:

- The performer's level of arousal.
- The stage of learning a performer is at.
- The level of anxiety a performer is experiencing.
- The previous experience of the performer.
- The time available to make a response.

CfE focus

By working as a group trying to identify different aspects of performance you are demonstrating you are developing the ability to become a **responsible citizen**. Working together to evaluate your own and other's performances shows that you can work collaboratively to solve problems and find more than one answer.

How does reaction time impact positively on performance?

In your own performance it would be an advantage to be first out of the blocks when sprinting and in gymnastics to react instantly to the feet touching the springboard when driving up to perform a somersault. Obviously being first away in a race means you instantly gain confidence and can start opening up a gap for the other competitors to try to close.

In volleyball, a cover player might need to react instantly to the ball deflecting off the block onto his own court. These quick reactions mean you can very quickly see what needs attention. This demands good concentration and the ability to shut out things which are irrelevant and do not require immediate attention, e.g. the crowd.

At the highest level, performers are trying to anticipate an opponent's next move. So in the volleyball example given previously in this chapter the cover player would anticipate that the spike **might** be deflected off the block and will make himself ready to move in any direction quickly. His body language will show that he is at the highest state of readiness. This body language will include things like being in a position ready to move, eyes focused on where the ball/opponent is, a look of concentration on his face. You might also be able to notice if a performer is calm and ready for anything that might happen – at breaks in the activity is the performer able to relax and prepare for what might come next?

GO! Activity

Look at the photograph of Roger Federer. What clues do you see which show that he is calm and in control? Make a graphic organiser adding all the body language clues you can see which might indicate his state of mind.

State of mind and reaction time

The state of mind a player can get into will have an impact on reaction times when participating. By being able to focus on playing, dancing, competing and shutting out all unnecessary distractions, a player can 'zoom in' on the things about the performance that need attention. Watch your opponent's body language – it might give you clues about what she is going to do. This means you can prepare for what you think she **might** be going to do. This will hopefully mean your reactions are 'lightning' fast.

In netball, the readiness and good awareness of the wing defence might mean she sees the goal attack signalling for an overhead pass into a space near where she is standing. If she waits for the right time to react to the pass that she anticipates the goal attack is **going** to receive, then she will probably successfully intercept it.

In badminton quick reactions enable a player to see the signs that an opponent is preparing to play an overhead disguised drop shot. A skilled player would then anticipate that quick movement into the net is needed for a return smash.

In dance, quick reactions might relate to something unexpected happening with a partner. This situation would require quick thinking and reactions to decide perhaps to take an extra step towards the partner in order to be able to complete the next lift together.

How do poor reactions impact negatively on performance?

A performer with poor reactions is slow to react to any stimulus. So in a game of football a player might be caught off guard by an approaching attacker who has broken through the defence unexpectedly. Slow reactions mean the player can wrongfoot him and skip past him towards goal.

Slow reactions from a football goalkeeper would mean an unexpected shot from a distance might catch them unready.

GO! Activity

Take some photos of people within your class engaged in different performances. Display photos that illustrate a good state of readiness.

GO! Activity

Look at the hockey goalkeeper in the video clip http://youtube/oojU9PAQGtk. Each time he makes the save he gets up as quickly as possible to be ready for a striker running in to take advantage of the ball being loose. If he were not ready then an easy goal-scoring opportunity would be given away.

Slow reactions can result in you losing points quickly in a competitive situation. In racquet sports slow reactions when moving around the court can result in the opponent using disguise to make you think the ball or shuttle is going in one direction when actually it is going in the opposite direction. Often in these circumstances, a player on the receiving end of this type of exploitation by an opponent gets very frustrated and this then impacts on their mental and emotional states of mind. This leads to bad decision-making, loss of concentration, anger and upset.

Make the link

Look at Chapter 5 on the emotional factor and at Chapter 6 on the mental factor. These chapters will remind you what happens when emotions impact on performance.

In creative activities, slow reactions mean mistakes can't be covered up and within the performance the **aesthetic appearance** is less successful.

✓ Assessment in PE

2.1 Describing strengths and areas for development in a performance.

Reaction time might be a strength or development need in your performance. To achieve this standard you have to describe what things are difficult for you, if your reactions are slow or, alternatively, what things you are able to do with good reaction times.

Activity

Look at the Gymnastics Falls Montage on YouTube (www. youtube.com/ watch?v=sMh3bFkVsXs).

How do I gather information on reaction time?

Most methods that exist to measure reaction time are based on the ability of your eyes to see and then respond to a stimulus. In the most well-known test – the ruler reaction test – the subject has to react to a ruler being dropped by trying to catch it as quickly as possible.

🔵 Activity

In this test the subject sits near the edge of a table resting their elbow on it so that their wrist is clear over the side of the table. The tester holds the ruler, allowing it to hang between the subject's thumb and index finger. The tester makes sure the point at zero on the ruler is in line with the top of the finger. The subject tells the tester when they are ready to begin the test. The tester then lets the ruler drop without warning and the subject must catch it as quickly as possible. The point on the ruler where it is caught should be recorded. Repeat the test six times and calculate an average. Use the table below to record the results you obtain.

Date of test	Distance in centimetres ruler fell
Attempt 1	
Attempt 2	
Attempt 3	
Attempt 4	
Attempt 5	
Attempt 6	

Average distance … centimetres

Appropriateness of the methods of data collection

This test is a standardised fitness test. This means the way it is carried out is exactly the same everywhere in the world. This gives a great deal of reliability. It means you can confidently compare your results to those of other class members, to those in a neighbouring school or even to a school in another city. As these tests have clear instructions (protocols) about how they are carried out it means when you retest yourself after training you should be able to see if your programme of work has been effective in bringing about any improvements to your reaction time.

✔ Assessment in PE

1.1 Explaining in detail two methods used to identify factors impacting on performance.

All the stages of this test will need to be explained if you are to achieve this assessment standard.

Preparation for performance development

There are some scientists who say reaction time is an ability you are born with and that only small improvements can be made to it through training.

However, most sports coaches and teachers believe reaction time training can be an important part of an overall training programme to improve overall performance.

Again, this aspect of skill-related fitness would probably not be the only focus for performance development. Rather it would be part of training targets set for a performer who might be finely tuning their training to try to get the edge on fellow competitors.

The form of training or approach used to develop reaction time includes using drills where the performer has to move quickly on a cue from an unfamiliar position to perform a familiar skill.

For example, a volleyball player might begin lying face down and when he hears the shout 'now' he must jump up and play the ball being fed to him. This drill could be adapted to help with football.

A badminton player might use smash drills, where she is required to constantly react to the smash from **two** opponents. This builds quick reactions as the player tries to spot the shuttle coming at her and tries to play it back as quickly as possible.

When devising a plan to develop this aspect of fitness it is necessary to try to keep the drills specific to the activity you are trying to improve.

A programme that is interesting and varied will ensure that boredom is not an issue. The focus should be to try to make small improvements in reaction time, adding to the work being done in an overall programme of work.

Approaches that impact positively on performance

Whichever collection of reaction time drills you use, you will need to make sure you are warmed up and able to move without fear of injury.

Drills where you move from an unfamiliar position to play a shot or return a feed are useful because they add an element of the unexpected to the execution of the skill.

Although there might **not** be occasions in your performance where you begin lying face down, the experience of moving from a position which is unusual to one that is familiar will be useful as the brain has to work very quickly to help you decide what to do next.

Fact

Sprinters are said to have had a 'false start' if their foot pushes back on the starting blocks within 0·10 seconds of the starter's gun going off. Usain Bolt has one of the slowest reaction times of his fellow competitors – around 0·16 compared to 0·13 and 0·14 of the other athletes. Yet he still beats them when he begins to run and holds the world record of 9·58 seconds for 100 metres.

In this type of situation you are forcing your brain and body to work together cooperatively and as quickly as possible.

When this experience is transferred into a real performance situation you should be able to react to the unexpected much more quickly.

🔵 Activity

Design a drill that forces you to get into position quickly to play a pass or strike a ball.

Draw the drill out and attempt to share your ideas with other members of your class.

✔ Assessment in PE

1.3 Explaining two approaches to develop performance.

2.3 Selecting and applying two approaches to impact positively on a performance.

The types of drills you design and use for this reaction time training will need to be explained in order to achieve this assessment standard.

Principles of training summary: reaction time

Frequency	Intensity	Duration	Progressive overload	Specificity
As part of an overall performance development programme.	As fast as you can move or react.	5–10 minutes.	Increase the number of things requiring you to react.	Include drills that use the types of reactions required for your focus activity.

Monitoring and evaluating

By keeping a note of the training you are doing you should start to **feel** a difference in the way you react while doing these drills. You could do this by using a training diary. As the drills and the unfamiliar positions become familiar, your body and brain learn what is required of them and react much more quickly. It could be said that they learn or anticipate what to do.

Your feeder should be able to give you information about changes they observe as they supply you with feeds. The accuracy of the pass or shot you manage to play might increase too as you become familiar with the movement patterns you are working on in these reaction time drills. See Chapter 8 for an example of how you could complete this training diary.

This will let you draw conclusions about the training you have completed and also about whether you have been successful in improving your overall performance.

Therefore, as well as retesting using the ruler reaction test, you must also look at your observations of your overall performance to see if you are quicker to react to the variety of stimuli you come across in your activity.

This would indicate how worthwhile your training has been and also would help you identify any new performance issues.

☑ Assessment in PE

3.2 Evaluating the effectiveness of the personal development plan in supporting performance development.

3.3 Evaluating progress based on all information gathered.

By completing the above processes you should be able to achieve the assessment standard required. You will need to comment on any improvements you see in your reaction time. Also, you should try to reflect back on the training you did and make a judgement about how useful this was in improving your overall performance.

Future needs
Within a well-balanced training programme it is likely some element of reaction time training might be included. This would ensure continued progress in this aspect of skill fitness.

Check your progress

Complete the following to check your understanding.

	HELP NEEDED	GETTING THERE	CONFIDENT
1. Give two examples of how quick reactions might help you in an activity of your choice.	◯	◯	◯
2. Give an example of when slow reactions might cause you problems in an activity.	◯	◯	◯
3. Describe how you would set up the ruler drop test.	◯	◯	◯
4. Explain a drill you could use to improve reaction time for an activity of your choice.	◯	◯	◯
5. Explain why you must monitor the progress you were making while trying to improve your reaction time.	◯	◯	◯

Make a judgement – were you able to complete these easily? If not, go back and look over some of the explanations or speak to your teacher for further advice.

3 The physical factor: aspects of skills and techniques

This chapter deals with aspects of skills and techniques that have an impact on your performance.

The features we are learning to identify and develop are:

- Nature of the activity
- Skills classification
- Skills and skilled performance
- Stages of learning

In this chapter you will learn:

1. How these features can impact on performance.
2. How to gather information: observation schedules, scatter diagrams, digital analysis, coach feedback.
3. How to prepare for performance development: goal-setting, work-to-rest ratio, model performance, work-to-rest ratio, duration/boredom, intensity of your practice, motivation, feedback, concentration.
4. Approaches to developing performance: types of training programmes, types of practice – shadow, repetition, feeder, opposed/unopposed, pressure, combination, conditioned games.

🧠 What should I already know?

During your broad general education you will have developed a range of skills for different activities. During this time you will have had the opportunity to try out different methods of training and you will have received continual feedback on your performance.

Feature of the factor: nature of the activity

There are a number of key questions for you to consider.

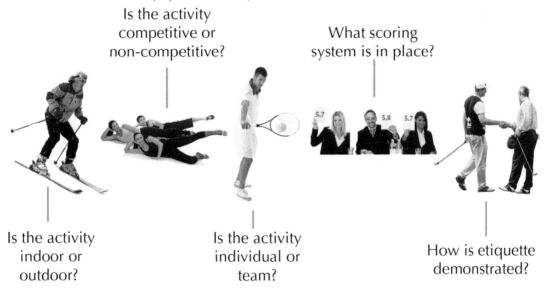

Is the activity competitive or non-competitive?

What scoring system is in place?

Is the activity indoor or outdoor?

Is the activity individual or team?

How is etiquette demonstrated?

How does the nature of the activity impact positively on performance?

Your personal strengths and weaknesses may dictate whether you are more suited to individual or team games or competitive or non-competitive activities.

You may perform better when you are working on your own to put together a dance composition or you may prefer to be part of a group working together to choreograph a dance. If you are working on your own in a non-competitive situation, you may be able to produce a more positive outcome.

The nature of the activity will impact on the performance you are able to give.

If an activity is outdoors then you may benefit from becoming skilled at adapting your performance to deal with changing weather conditions.

In a team setting there is shared responsibility and it might be that you are comfortable working with others to produce a good overall team performance.

Similarly, in individual activities you will be aware that all decisions are taken by you and you have no need to consult others about what you should do in a performance situation.

Competition can have a very positive impact on your performance and the excitement that it brings encourages many performers to participate in sport and physical activity. However, some activities are non-competitive and it is likely that you might just enjoy doing these activities for their own sake, e.g. going for a cycle with friends, going for a run or going to the golf range to practise your driving.

How does the nature of the activity impact negatively on your performance?

Perhaps you are more suited to a slower-paced game or an individual activity. Perhaps you like working on your own and struggle to work within a team. If you find yourself in either of these situations they may have a detrimental effect on your performance, as you struggle to communicate with others in your team.

Feature of the factor: skills classification

Simple skills

Simple skills are straightforward and require little concentration or ability, e.g. jumping, striking, passing.

Complex skills

Complex skills involve a lot more concentration and can be more difficult to perform. They may involve difficult movement patterns, e.g. handspring, lay up, spike.

Open skills

Open skills are ones in which the environment can constantly change and you must be able to adapt the skills you have depending on the situation, e.g. a football pass can be affected by your position, the position of other players or the playing conditions. All of these aspects will impact on your performance positively or negatively.

Closed skills

Closed skills are performed in an environment where you solely focus on the skills and you are not usually affected by other aspects of the performance, e.g. a free throw in basketball is a closed skill, as there are few distractions.

	How does this skill impact positively on my performance?	How does this skill impact negatively on my performance?
Simple skills	You don't have to think too much when carrying them out so you can concentrate on other aspects of your performance.	May limit the performer – simple skills may not be as effective in certain performance situations. Sometimes it is necessary for the performer to carry out more complex skills, which results in their performance improving. If the performer is only able to carry out simple skills this will have a negative impact on their performance.
Complex skills	If you are able to carry out some complex skills in a performance you will be able to cope with the various demands of that performance. For example, in basketball, if you can perform a lay-up with either hand, you have more scoring options in the game.	If you are unable to perform complex skills within a performance, you may limit your potential. You may come across situations where using a more complex skill would enhance your performance.
Open skills	Being able to perform an open skill consistently will allow you to cope much better with the external demands of your performance.	When performing an open skill it is essential that you can cope with external factors, which may be constantly changing. If not, this can have a negative impact on your performance.
Closed skills	If you are practising a closed skill, this can benefit your performance as you only have to consider the technique of your closed skill. This is particularly important in the early stages of learning, so that the performer has a better opportunity to concentrate fully on how to perform the skill.	If a closed skill is practised in closed conditions for too long, progress could be very limited. This will mean it is difficult to make use of the skill in a more challenging context. For example, in a competitive situation.

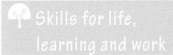 Skills for life, learning and work

By completing this table you are developing investigative skills where you are making decisions based on the knowledge you have about different activities. This type of project makes you think about what is involved and to put these into categories to help you make sense of the way skills and techniques are developed.

GO! Activity

Make a table of all the different activities you carry out in your course or outside school.

On this table select different skills and categorise them as either simple/complex or open/closed. An example has been filled in for you. Make the table as big as you need it to be.

Activity	Skills/techniques	Classification
Gymnastics	Forward roll	Closed simple

You may wish to try out some of these skills/techniques, before you classify them.

111

Feature of the factor: skills and skilled performance

Your ability to perform skills and techniques within an activity will impact on your performance significantly. You may have a natural ability to perform some skills in specific activities or you may have to work hard to develop them. Your ability to both develop your skill level progressively and perform a range of skills within an activity will impact on your whole performance.

How does the ability to perform skills and techniques impact positively on performance?

For example, in badminton, if you are able to perform an overhead clear to the back tramlines and accurately place it to different parts on the court, this will impact on your performance positively as you can force your opponent to the back of the court and also move them to different areas of it. This would give you the advantage of being able to dictate play and in effect be in control of the game.

How does a lack of ability to perform skills and techniques impact negatively on performance?

For example, in basketball, if you are unable to dribble the ball with control, this will impact on your performance negatively as you are unable to dribble the ball successfully down the court, without either losing control or your opponent stealing the ball off you. This would mean your own and team's performance would be less effective.

Skills for life, learning and work

Throughout your life you will have to develop a range of skills, which will impact on your personal, social and professional life. Being able to develop these skills in a progressive and positive way will help you reach your targets.

Feature of the factor: stages of learning

Cognitive stage

At this stage you will have the opportunity to learn a new skill or perhaps go back to re-examine a previously learned skill. During this stage you will be looking to break down the skill to its most simple form or correct any errors. For example how you hold the racket, where you place your feet. At this stage you will receive lots of external feedback, so that any mistakes can be corrected.

Associative stage

At this stage you will be becoming quite comfortable with the skill, you will be making fewer errors and becoming more consistent. You will now be looking to practise the skill over and over again. This way you will be able to look at parts of the skill that need to be improved and correct any mistakes. You will need to receive external feedback, so that you will be more aware of any faults.

Automatic stage

At this stage you will be able to perform a skill without having to give it too much thought. You will focus less on the skill and be able to detect any errors yourself. This will mean you will have more time to focus on other aspects of your performance, e.g. what tactics you may wish to apply.

How do the stages of learning impact positively on performance?

The stage of learning you are performing at can impact your performance both positively and negatively. Being able to determine your stage of learning will allow you to select the most appropriate practice and receive appropriate feedback. For example, if you are in the cognitive stage for learning a handstand in gymnastics, it is important that you receive basic, specific feedback on how best to perform this skill.

How do stages of learning impact negatively on performance?

If you do not consider the stage of learning you are at, you may end up designing practices that are too difficult or not difficult enough. What would happen if you were at the cognitive stage of learning and you had to complete a complicated combination drill? Or if you were in the automatic stage of learning and were asked to use a shadow practice, how would you feel?

✔ Assessment in PE

1.2 Explaining in detail the impact of one positive and one negative factor on performance.

You may wish to consider some of the information on the previous pages to help you gather evidence for your FIP assessment standard. You can explore these different features and try to think how they might impact on your performance in your selected activity.

GO! Activity

The diagram below shows the impact having a poor backhand clear in badminton has on your performance.

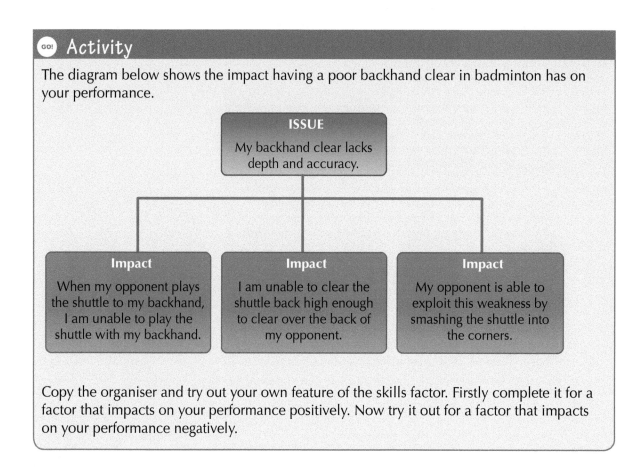

Copy the organiser and try out your own feature of the skills factor. Firstly complete it for a factor that impacts on your performance positively. Now try it out for a factor that impacts on your performance negatively.

How do I gather information about this factor?

Within the skills factor you will need to have an understanding of how to collect information on your performance, as well as explaining why you may use these methods. Here are some methods you may wish to use and why they may be beneficial.

General observation schedule

A GOS allows you to gather information on a range of skills and movement patterns and makes it easy for you to compare them against qualitative statements. An observer either records the information on the schedule during the performance or they may digitally record the performance and complete the schedule afterwards.

General observation schedule

PERFORMER'S NAME:_____

OBSERVER'S NAME:_____

	Skill/movement pattern	Often	Sometimes	Never
Range of skills	E.g. Forehand			
Movement patterns	E.g. Movement in attack			
Decision-making	E.g. Making the right decisions when under pressure			

Analyse your data. What does it suggest? Identify the specific strengths and weaknesses of your whole game performance in relation to the information you have gathered.

Focused observation schedule

This schedule allows you to break down a specific skill into sub-routines for the preparation, action and recovery phases.

Preparation → Get ready to perform the skill

Action → Carry out the performance of the skill

Recovery → Get ready to carry out the next skill

The observer records performance against qualitative statements either during the performance or after via a digital recording.

Focused observation schedule

✓ = successful, X = needs development

PERFORMER'S NAME_____

OBSERVER'S NAME_____

DATE_____

Stage of skill	How it should be performed	First observation	Second observation after practice
Preparation	E.g Ready to strike ball		
Action	E.g. Striking the ball with inside of foot		
Recovery	E.g. Getting back into the ready position		

Scatter diagram/notation

A scatter diagram allows an observer to plot the range of shots used within a game, identifying them as a strength or a weakness.

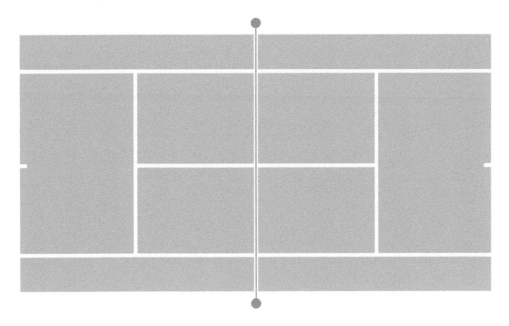

Notation key

FD – forehand drive: x✓   SS – second serve: x✓

BD – backhand drive: x✓   D – drop: x✓

FV – forehand volley: x✓   S – smash: x✓

BV – backhand volley: x✓   x = unsuccessful

FS – first serve: x✓   ✓ =successful

Digital analysis

It may be possible for your performance to be recorded digitally and stored. You may choose to use a digital recorder or perhaps you could use your mobile. Make sure you that you clearly capture your performance so that you can watch it back again.

Coach feedback

Receiving feedback, whether written or verbal, from your coach, teacher or peer will occur throughout your performance. It is always important to listen to this feedback so that you can make changes to your performance.

It is important that you are able to collect information as accurately as possible. This will help you with the reliability and validity of your data. Make sure you set up an appropriate performance situation, where the context you are performing in gives a full picture of your abilities.

Methods of data collection

Methods can be:

- Visual, clearly showing your strengths and weaknesses.

- Specifically designed to highlight the parts of the skill you need to work on, which will help you when you are planning your programme of work.

- Digitally recorded, allowing you to use slow motion, pause, replay, frame-by-frame images, which all help you gather accurate information.

- Used straightaway so that you gain instant feedback on your performance.

- Stored and used to compare your performance when required.

✔Assessment in PE

1.1 Explaining in detail two methods used to identify factors impacting on performance or 'planning personal performance' in your portfolio.

You may wish to consider some of the information on the previous page to help you gather evidence to link to the assessment standard.

Look at some of the examples and see how they might help you to explain methods of collecting data on skills within your performance. Now try to think about how you may want to use these methods to gather information on your performance in your chosen activity.

GO! Activity

Select an activity.

Complete the table below to plan out how you will collect information on your skills and techniques.

1. How will I collect information on my whole performance?	
2. Within Skills, what feature do I want to focus on, i.e. which skill feature impacts on my performance?	
3. How will I collect information on this feature?	
4. How will I record the results generated using this method?	Description:

5. Is the equipment I need available?	Yes	No

6. How will I use these methods of data collection?

Skills for life, learning and work

In some of your other subjects, you will have been given the task of collecting information, perhaps to record the results of an experiment in Science or when you are processing information in Maths. These types of skill will help you transfer your knowledge from subject to subject.

During your level 3 and 4 broad and general physical education course you will have been given opportunities to evaluate and appreciate your own and your peer group's performances. For example, you may have recorded your performance on a flip camera and watched it back or you may have been asked to watch a classmate and offer some suggestions on how they might improve.

Preparation for performance development

Before you consider approaches that will impact positively on your performance, you must devise a plan of action to help you achieve your targets. You will most likely develop a programme of work. Before you start you should consider the following:

- Goal-setting
- Model performance
- Work-to-rest ratio
- Progression of practices: duration/boredom
- Intensity of practice
- Motivation
- Feedback
- Concentration

Goal-setting

Long-term goals will be set to help you consider what you want to achieve over a specific period of time. You should set short-term goals to help you reach your longer-term goal.

Specific goal-setting	Are the goals specific to the performer, their ability, the activity?
Measurable goal-setting	Can you measure whether you are meeting your goals or not?
Achievable goal-setting	Can you achieve and attain these goals?
Realistic goal-setting	Do you have the ability and resources to realistically achieve these goals?
Time-based goal-setting	Do you have enough time to achieve these goals?
Exciting goals	Are the goals you have set yourself exciting? Do they motivate you? Do they give you a sense of accomplishment?
Recording goal-setting	Are you able to record your progress, so that you can monitor and evaluate?

Model performance

A model performance will give you an exact image of how a skill should be performed. It will allow you to compare your own performance and identify strengths and development needs. It is also a useful way of collecting information.

Models of performances are crucial when developing your skills and techniques. They can inspire you by making the performances look more exciting and challenging. This will then help you with your own motivation and potentially increase your determination to improve. Using digital devices now gives you an opportunity to compare your own performance against a model performance, where you can slow performances down, freeze frame them and watch the performances back. Many apps now allow you to watch two performances side by side, for example Coach's Eye.

Work-to-rest ratio

It is important to make sure you build enough rest in between your practices and your practice sessions. This way you will be able to focus on which areas to improve, rather than losing interest or becoming too tired. You will need to consider how long your practices have to be and how much rest to give yourself in between practices.

Progression of practices

You must make sure your practices are progressive so that you can improve your skill gradually. Make sure you start with simple practices, building to more challenging practices, where you are able to work on specific weakness.

For example you might want to make your practices progress by adding an opponent, or performing the skill under some type of pressure.

Duration/boredom

You need to make sure your practices are as exciting and enjoyable as possible to avoid boredom. When you enjoy a practice you are far more likely to see improvements and see the relevance of that practice.

Consider your own practices. Do you perform better at the start of the session? Do you lose concentration if a practice goes on too long?

Intensity of practice

Remember you need to work hard to improve your skill level. The quality of your practices will be crucial in making any improvements. If you feel that your intensity is dropping, think about taking a break and then returning to the practice.

Getting the best out of your practices will give you the best possible results. You need determination, concentration and a strong desire to improve.

Motivation

There are two types of motivation: internal and external.

> ### ☀ Make the link
>
> Refer to Chapter 6, The mental factor, and read about 'level of arousal'.

Internal motivation

How motivated you are will be determined by your own personality and whether you have the ambition to succeed in your selected performances. Throughout your performances you will need to have a strong desire to improve and to do your very best in all performance situations. Setting short- and long-term goals may help.

External motivation

Receiving external rewards such as medals and prize money can help your motivation.

For example, during your golf performance, thinking about winning medals during your club competitions may help motivate you to do your very best.

Benefits of high levels of motivation

A performer who is highly motivated will always have greater success when developing their skill level. A motivated performer will face any challenges positively and will always strive to improve. They will also lead by example, helping other performers to reach their own goals.

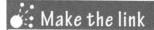

Make the link

How motivated are you across your subject areas? Make a list of your favourite subjects. Are you always motivated to do well? What drives your motivation?

GO! Activity

Make a list of the subjects you cover at school. Give yourself a score from 1 to 5 (1 being the best) to describe how motivated you feel in that class. Now make a comment on how you came to that score.

Subject	How motivated are you?	How do you know?
English	4	I don't seem to be able to concentrate.

Feedback

There are two types of feedback – internal and external. All feedback received should be (where possible) given straight away. Make sure that the feedback you receive is as exact and detailed as possible, allowing you to continually make changes to your performance.

Internal feedback

Being able to sense your own body movements or checking how you perform a particular skill will help you examine whether you are carrying out the skill correctly or not. You will be able to feel whether you have completed the skill correctly or not, e.g. how did I feel when I landed my vault securely? Did I feel whether I was side on before I played my overhead clear?

External feedback

Receiving external feedback from a variety of sources, such as a teacher, coach, fellow pupil or demonstration is crucial to improving your performance. You should always think about starting with something positive within the performance when giving feedback, perhaps some encouragement or some recognition of the parts of the skill that the performer is carrying out well. Follow this by highlighting some specific points or areas of the skill that need to be developed. Encouragement is always important in your performance.

Benefits of feedback

Receiving good quality feedback always helps and motivates the performer to improve. You should always be able to see whether any improvements have been made and what areas you should be working on next. This is especially important when you are in the cognitive stage, where it is essential that you receive good quality external feedback to ensure that you are performing the skill with the correct techniques.

Concentration

When practising you must try to concentrate on the exact parts of the skill you are looking to improve upon. It is important that your mind is set and ready for performance, but this is also equally important when carrying out practice sessions. Again, this is crucial during the cognitive stage of learning, when it is important that you learn the skill correctly.

 **Make the link**

You may wish to refer to the Chapter 6, The mental factor, where we look at concentration in more detail.

☑ **Assessment in PE**

2.1 Describing strengths and areas for development in a performance.

2.2 Preparing and implementing a personal development plan containing clearly identified development targets or 'planning personal performance' in your portfolio.

You may wish to consider some of the features above to help you gather evidence to link to the assessment standard. Think about your own strengths and areas for development in your performance. Are you able to link a personal development plan to them in order to enhance your performance?

Look at the information on pages 120–123 and see how it might help you to plan your development of your skill level within your selected activity. Think about how you can plan a successful programme of work, using the principles of effective practice, goal-setting, motivation, concentration and feedback.

Approaches to develop performance

Deciding the approaches you want to take to help you impact on your performance positively should start with considering what type of sessions you want to carry out.

You may wish to consider planning your practice sessions quite intensely within a whole week, or you might want to carry out your practice session over a longer period of time. You may wish to develop your performance using a gradual build-up, where you move from simple practices to more challenging practices as you become more confident and accomplished, or whole-part-whole, where you practise all of the skill, then practise small sub-routines of the skill and then practise the whole skill again. An example of whole-part-whole would be using a feeder practice to practise the overhead clear, then using a shadow practice to work on the transfer of weight, then practising the whole skill again with a feeder practice.

The methods below are approaches which will help you to develop your skills, and which you can incorporate into your training programme for your FIP or your portfolio.

The table below will help you understand what they are and how they are useful.

What methods of practice will you use?	Why will you use this method of practice?
Shadow practice This is where you have to shadow the movements of your skill, e.g. when practising your footwork for forehand drive in tennis you shadow the movement without any equipment.	• You can learn the skill without putting yourself under pressure. • You can focus on the feedback you receive.
Feeder practices This is where you use a feeder to repeatedly feed to a specific area every time. This is repeated several times, e.g. 10 times with a rest, then repeat.	• You are able to consider the feedback you receive after every feed. • You are able to control the depth and pace of the feed. • For some practices you can self-feed.
Repetition/drills This is where you will repeat the same action over and over again. E.g. in basketball you can practise passing the ball repeatedly with a partner.	• You are able to practise the parts of the skill that are causing problems. • You can improve on the parts of the skill that are flawed. • You will be able to increase your confidence. • You will become more consistent.
Pressure training Throughout the practice session, you can make sure you add some pressure training. For example, you may consider changing the speed of the practice or the type of opposition.	• You will be able to make the practices more like the experience of performing. • Your practices will be more realistic. • You will be able to make your practices more exciting.

What methods of practice will you use?	Why will you use this method of practice?
Conditioned games performances Sometimes you can change the rules or the conditions of a performance to highlight a specific skill. For example, in football, you may want to change your passing game to two touches to concentrate more on your control.	• Your practice will reflect the actual performance. • You will have to make quick decisions and respond speedily. • You are able to focus on a specific part of your skill within your performance.
Unopposed/opposed practice During this practice you can start with no opposition, and then opposition can be gradually introduced.	• You are able to practise your skill with passive opposition. • You can gradually increase opposition, which allows you to gain more confidence.
Combination drills During this drill you can carry out specific skills in order, e.g. in squash: serve, backhand drive, forehand drive and repeat.	• This allows you to combine specific skills. • You can find these practices far more challenging. • It feels more game-like.

✔ Assessment in PE

1.3 Explaining two approaches to develop performance.

2.2 Preparing and implementing a personal development plan containing clearly identified development targets.

2.3 Selecting and applying two approaches to impact positively on a performance or 'planning, developing and implementing approaches to enhance personal performance' in your portfolio.

You may wish to consider some of these features to help you gather evidence for your FIP link to the assessment standard. Think about the goals you have set yourself. What training methods did you use? Did they have a positive impact on your performance?

Check your progress

Complete the following to check your understanding.

	HELP NEEDED	GETTING THERE	CONFIDENT
1. What do you consider to be the main features within Skills that impact on your performance?	◯	◯	◯
2. How have you been able to gather information on these features?	◯	◯	◯
3. What do you have to consider when planning to improve your performance?	◯	◯	◯
4. What approaches to development have you used?	◯	◯	◯
5. What impact have these approaches had on your performance?	◯	◯	◯

Make a judgement – were you able to complete these easily? If not, go back and look over some of the explanations or speak to your teacher for further advice.

4 The physical factor: strategy, formation and/or composition

This chapter deals with all the strategy, formation and/or composition (SFC) features that you will need to consider before any performance.

The features we are learning to identify and develop are:

- Individual and team/group strengths/weaknesses
- Roles and responsibilities
- Performance conditions
- Fundamentals of strategy, formation and/or composition
- Principles of play – attack and defence
- Choreographic devices

In this chapter you will learn:

1. How strategy, formation and/or composition features can impact on performance: strengths and weaknesses, roles and responsibilities, performance conditions, SFC fundamentals, principles of attack and defence, choreographic devices.

2. How to gather information: match analysis, digital analysis, coach feedback, self-reflection.

3. How to prepare for performance development: individual and team strengths and weaknesses, opponents' strengths and weaknesses, performance conditions, roles and responsibilities, strategy, formation and/or composition fundamentals.

4. To understand and apply approaches to developing performance: adapting/changing strategy, formation and/or composition, practice sessions.

What should I already know?

From your broad general education you will have some knowledge of:

- The different tactics used in some activities.
- The range of structures that can be used in team games.

What is strategy, formation and /or composition?

Strategy, formation and/or composition is a plan of action an individual or a team/group may take on to achieve a specific goal.

In your performance, whether as an individual or in a team game, dance or gymnastic performance, you must always have a plan for how you can best achieve your goal of winning or performing at your best.

Here are some examples of strategy, formation and/or composition.

Type	Activity	SFC
Team	Football	4–4–2 Formation
Individual	Badminton	Exploiting opponent's weakness in playing a shot to the back of the court
Creative	Dance	Binary, ternary, rondo or narrative

It may be useful (although not one of the assessment standards you have to achieve) to think about how to describe a strategy, formation and/or composition.

Some examples have been given below.

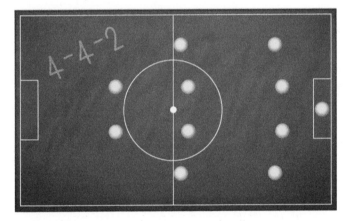

Football

In football a formation you may want to use might be the 4–4–2. The 4-4-2 is made up of four defenders, four midfielders and two strikers. The defenders' role is to stop your opponents penetrating any dangerous areas. The midfielders' role is to look to set up attacks and support in defence – they are always looking to make space and exploit opponents. The strikers are always trying to work together to take opportunities to stretch their opponent's defence, and to take shots at goal.

Badminton

In badminton a strategy might be to force your opponent to the back court, as you know they are weak at returning the shuttlecock deep into your half. They normally only manage to place the shuttlecock mid court, therefore you are able to use your smash to win a point.

Dance

In dance a composition might be to use narrative form, choreographic devices and motif development to unfold a story to the audience.

🔵 Activity

In the space below write up or draw your selected strategy, formation and/or composition.

Activity:

My selected strategy, formation and/or composition is

Feature of the factor: individual and team/group strengths/weaknesses

Identification of individual strengths and weaknesses (your own or an opponent's) is crucial to the formation of strategy.

The identification of individual strengths and weaknesses must be completed before any performance so that any particular circumstance that might come up can be dealt with quickly, and with as much success as possible.

You might have to consider the strengths and weaknesses of:

- ☑ your own individual performance
- ☑ your team's performance
- ☑ your opponent's performance.

How do strengths and weaknesses impact positively on performance?

If you are aware of your own strengths and weaknesses, you will be able to pre-plan to exploit your strengths and try to counteract any weaknesses. For example, in badminton a strength of your performance might be your ability to play an accurate overhead clear consistently to the back of the court. This will allow you to force your opponent to the back of the court, giving you more time to think about your next shot.

How do strengths and weaknesses impact negatively on performance?

During a centre pass strategy in netball, if a centre cannot control the ball at speed this may have a negative impact on performance, as the ball will not be moved up the court quickly. This will have an impact on the whole team's performance of the strategy, as the ball may not be able to be received by the next free player.

✔ Assessment in PE

1.2 Explaining in detail the impact of one positive and one negative factor on performance or 'understanding factors that impact on performance' in your portfolio.

You may wish to consider some of the features above to help you gather evidence to link to this assessment standard. Take a couple of these features and explain the positive or negative impact that they might have on your strategy, formation and/or composition.

GO! Activity

Activity 1

Complete the table below, identifying the strengths and weaknesses of strategy, formation and/or composition. Make some suggestions of the impact the identified strengths and weaknesses may have on your performance.

Activity	Strengths	Weaknesses	Impact on performance
Team			
Individual			
Creative			

Activity 2

Before your performance, either on your own or in a small group, take some time to discuss the strengths and weaknesses of your strategy, formation and/or composition.
Consider any strengths and weaknesses of your own or your opponent's performance afterwards as well.
Here are some key questions you may wish to consider.

	Comments
What are your own individual strengths and weaknesses?	
What are your own key strengths and weaknesses in your chosen dance form and selected choreographic devices? Or What are your team's key strengths and weaknesses in your chosen strategy in your team game?	
What are your opponent's strengths and weaknesses?	
Did you have to consider making any changes during your performance to help with any identified strengths and weaknesses?	

Add some more questions of your own.

Feature of the factor: roles and responsibilities

Before you decide on any strategy, formation and/or composition and decisions related to who might carry out the various roles, you should consider:

The demands of the activity:
'Do I understand motif development and the use of choreographic devices in my composition?'

'Am I able to design a dance composition within the time restrictions?'

The demands of the role:
'Am I able to shoot with consistency, in my role as goal shooter?'

'Am I aware of the demands of a choreographer to deliver my vision?'

How your opponent's ability affects your choice of strategy.

'My opponent has a strong smash, am I able to use a defensive shot effectively?'

Personal demands:
'As captain, am I able to keep control of my emotions if we go into extra time?'

Within any performance you must have a sound knowledge of your role within your strategy, formation and/or composition and your key responsibilities. How effectively you carry out your role/responsibilities will have a significant impact on the overall success of the strategy, formation and/or composition. For example, in your group dance your role may be to mirror the movements of the other dancers. You will have to make sure that your movements are exact and carefully timed. This will have a positive impact on your performance, as the dance will flow and be more fluent.

CfE focus

Taking on the responsibility of a specific role will allow you to discover the different life skills needed to face the challenge. This will help you to work with others and become a responsible citizen.

 **Make the link**

During your level 3 and level 4 courses you will have had to take on a role or a responsibility for a particular task. Think back and consider what you had to do in order to complete that role.

How does your role or responsibility impact positively on performance?

In basketball, if the guard can move the ball down the court with control and speed, your team will have a better opportunity to outnumber the defence, which may lead to an unopposed drive to the basket and hopefully more baskets on target.

How does your role or responsibility impact negatively on performance?

If, in hockey, during your short corner strategy, your centre midfielder does not have enough power and accuracy to push the ball at the short corner to the stopper, your strategy will not be carried out with pace and therefore your opponents will have longer to react.

GO! Activity

Using the example above, select another team activity and consider the demands of the activity, the strategy, formation and/or composition, the role you play and the impact it can have on your opponents or your performance.

Activity demands	
Strategy, formation and/or composition	
My role/responsibility:	
Impact on opponents or performance:	

Feature of the factor: performance conditions

The conditions you are faced with before, during and after your performance will also have an impact on your performance. These conditions may include:

- Weather or ground conditions
- The facility you are performing in
- The time in the performance
- The score in a game
- Your own or your team's previous experience

How do performance conditions impact positively or negatively on performance?

Weather/ground conditions

For example, in golf the wind will determine the direction, speed and trajectory of your drive. This may have a positive or negative impact on your performance, especially when you are considering where to place the ball.

The facility

The facility you perform in will also have an impact on your performance. In dance, when considering your composition, you will have to decide on how to best use the space to make sure you have a positive impact. This will require careful consideration of the movement used within the composition.

Time

You may only have a short period of time during a creative performance. You must make sure that you put the correct level of effort within that time frame.

Or how can slowing your game down, especially if you are ahead, impact on your performance?

Score

You may have to consider the time in a performance, for example you may be winning in netball by only one goal – how do you make sure your opponents don't have another successful attacking opportunity?

Previous experience

What experience do you or your team have? Have you just started performing, or do you have a new player taking on a new role within a strategy, formation and/or composition.

 Skills for life, learning and work

In a situation where you are dependent on others, skills for life, learning and work are being developed. In the world of work, you will find many situations where you need to communicate with others to help you complete a task. Being able to communicate and cooperate with others to get a job done means you are using inter-personal skills.

✔Assessment in PE

1.2 Explaining in detail the impact of one positive and one negative factor on performance or 'understanding factors that impact on performance' in your portfolio.

You may wish to consider some of the features above to help you gather evidence to link to the assessment standard. Take a couple of these and explain the positive or negative impact that they might have on your strategy, formation and/or composition.

Feature of the factor: fundamentals of strategy, formation and/or composition

Within any performance, having an understanding of key fundamentals of strategy, formation and/or composition will have a definite impact on your performance.

Here are some of the key fundamentals of strategy or formation and how they may impact on your performance.

Space

Being able to use space within your strategy, formation and/or composition is crucial. It will allow you to get the best out of your attack and close down space when defending. Performers must have good spatial awareness so that they can use space effectively.

Being able to use space effectively can have a positive impact on performance where players are able to move into and create space to allow teammates to keep possession of the ball.

Pressurising opponents

Being able to pressurise your opponents within your strategy, formation and/or composition will give you opportunities to force your opponents to make mistakes, by denying them time. There are various methods of applying pressure in game situations. For example, placing a double team on an opponent, using speed in your defence, always pressurising an opponent's weak skill.

Being able to apply pressure can have a positive impact on your performance by, for example, leading to you quickly turning a defensive situation into an attacking option.

Tactical elements

Tactics apply to the specific way you wish to carry out your strategy, formation and/or composition. This will very much be determined by your pre-plan, where you will need to consider the playing conditions, your opponent's strengths and weaknesses and your own strengths and weaknesses. During the performance you may choose to change your tactics due to an injury, the time left in the performance or a specific problem with your strategy/formation.

Speed

As mentioned earlier, speed is important when defending to apply pressure to your opponents. However speed is also crucial when attacking. Using speed in ball games to speed up the pace of your attacking options in your strategy, formation and/or composition will allow you to move the ball quickly and create more space.

GO! Activity

Think back and consider different performances you have been involved in. Make a list of any tactics you have had to consider before your performance. Give a reason why these tactics were necessary.

Sometimes a lack of speed can have a positive impact on your performance. For example, by slowing down a game you are narrowly winning towards the end, you can keep possession of the ball and help to achieve a positive outcome.

Decision-making

During your performance you must be able to make the correct decisions for the situation you find yourself in. This will allow you to apply solutions to any potential problems you may find yourself in within your strategy, formation and/or composition.

Being able to consider all the information and then apply the correct decision will have a positive impact on your performance. For example, in tennis being able to identify that your opponent's weakness is their backhand drive and your decision to play the ball as much as possible to their backhand will put pressure on your opponent. This can have a positive impact on your performance as you will be able to exploit this weakness, which may mean the difference between winning and losing the game.

On the other hand, bad decision-making can impact negatively on performance. In rugby, for example, a bad decision would be when the scrum half has the ball in an attacking two-on-one situation and decides not to pass the ball before being tackled – the scrum half will be tackled, in possession of the ball, and therefore a potential attacking situation will have been prevented.

✔ **Assessment in PE**

1.2 Explaining in detail the impact of one positive and one negative factor on performance in your FIP unit.

You may wish to consider some of the features above to help you gather evidence to link to the assessment standard. Look at some of the examples and see how they explain the positive or negative impact that they might have on the strategy, formation and/or composition.

Now consider your own strategy, formation and/or composition. How might these features impact on your performance? Make sure you can clearly explain how the features impact on your performance.

Feature of the factor: principles of play – attack and defence

When preparing for and carrying out your strategy and formation you should consider how applying the principles of play can have an impact on your performance.

Here are some of the fundamental principles of play in attack and defence.

Attack

Penetrate the defence
When you are in an attacking situation, you should always consider how you could penetrate the defence of your opponents. This may be through being able to create space or through changing the pace of your strategy or formation.

Support
During an attacking situation there should always be an option of support from your fellow players. Teammates should be able to move into a space that will allow you support options.

Width
Being able to use the width of your playing area will give you attacking options. Spreading your players across the area will create space; this will in turn spread the defence and stretch your opponents.

Depth
Having players in a position behind the attackers to support play will allow more cover and potentially create another attacking option.

Mobility
In your attack if you are able to move easily, using different speeds of runs, this will allow you to draw your opponents out of position and give you more attacking opportunities.

Defence

Delay
Being able to slow down your opponents' attack will allow you to take more control of the game. Applying pressure quickly to your opponents, by closing them down in defence, may lead to your opponents' attacking options being disrupted or even stopped. It will also give your teammates time to get back in defence.

Support
When defending there should always be a teammate offering support in case the first line of defence breaks down.

Awareness
Being able to focus and keep your concentration on your opponents' options will allow you to make the correct decisions throughout your performance. It is always important to give your full attention, especially at important times in the game.

How do these features impact positively on performance?

Having an awareness of the principles of play in attack and defence will allow you to have a better understanding of what your team needs to do in their formation or strategy. For example in hockey, if your team or individuals use the natural width in their 4-4-2 formation, it will allow more space to carry out the attack. This may lead to a positive outcome.

How do these features impact negatively on performance?

In basketball during your man-to-man defence, if some of your team members do not help support in defence, it may mean that your opponents are able to get past a player and have an easy option to score a basket. With no support from other defensive players to step in to help, your opponents will have an unopposed attacking option.

Composition/form: style

When considering dance form you will be looking at the structure of the dance. For example you may consider a narrative form, where your dance is telling a story, or you may consider binary form (a dance of one part), a dance in two parts, or a ternary form (a dance of three parts).

There are a range of dance styles you may wish to consider, such as jazz, modern or contemporary.

When working on your dance formation/composition you will require motif development. This is where you will develop movement patterns through using some of the choreographic devices as outlined on page 138. You may work on a single movement or a series of short movements to come up with a phrase of different motifs which all link together.

In other creative activities, such as gymnastics and trampoline, your formation/composition routine will be based around the movement and linking the patterns you use. Being able to use choreographic devices will help you plan your routine.

Feature of the factor: choreographic devices

When preparing for and carrying out your formation and/or composition you should consider how applying choreographic devices can have an impact on your performance.

Fundamental principles of choreographic devices

Floor patterns

During your routine/motif you should travel different floor paths. They may be straight, curved or a combination of these things. How you apply the most appropriate special pattern will have an impact on your performance, for how you move and how the dance appears to your audience. Using a variety of floor patterns such as diagonal lines, circle formations and spirals, will help you get across the message of your composition.

Partner work

Working with a partner can add an extra element to your composition. Dancing with a partner you will have to coordinate, time movements, and maintain eye contact so that the composition flows fluently. Working with a partner can impact positively on your performance, giving an extra dynamic to your composition. Using partner work in your composition adds a different dimension. It can allow you to develop relationships and portray feelings.

Levels

Different levels in your formation/composition – high, medium and low – can be explored through kneeling, standing, jumping or lying down. Using different levels can have a positive impact on your performance, allowing you to show a wider range of creativity in your movement and motif patterns. The use of levels will portray a special type of movement to your audience.

Flow

Being able to make your formation and/or composition flow will help create seamless, fluid movements, which will allow you to link parts of the dance with ease. This can impact on your performance, as it will allow you to make the transition easier and smoother. This, in turn, will look better to the audience.

Dynamics

Altering the dynamics of the movement will change the impact on the audience. Slowing down or changing the dynamics of a movement/movements can have a positive or negative impact on your performance.

Space

Using different levels and special patterns will help you use space more effectively in your formation and/or composition.

How do these features impact positively on performance?

Having an awareness of choreographic devices will allow you to plan your routine so that it uses the space effectively, so that the routine flows fluently and is also attractive to the audience. For example, in your trampoline routine being able to use skills and movements that link smoothly will give your routine a beautiful flow and make the transition of skills/movement much easier. This will have a positive impact on your performance because the impact of your routine on the audience will be much greater.

How do these features impact negatively on performance?

In a group dance, if the composition does not co-ordinate with other group members, the dance can lose its impact. The whole group routine may fall apart or some of the group may lose their place.

How do I gather information on these features?

It is crucial to gather information on your strategy, formation and/or composition before your performance. Below are some suggestions for gathering this vital information, so that the correct decisions can be made before and during the performance.

Match analysis
Completing a statistical analysis of the key points of your strategy, formation and/or composition can allow you to gather information on its key strengths and weaknesses.

Centre pass 1 C>WA>C>GA>GS>Score	C>WA	WA>C	C>GA	GA>GS	Score	% success
	✓	✓	✓	X	X	0%
Centre pass 2 C>GA>GS>GA>Score	C>GA	GA>GS	GS>GA		Score	% success
	✓	✓	✓		✓	100%

Digital analysis
There are many forms of digital analysis – have a look at Focus and Dartfish. These software programs and apps allow you to analyse every aspect of your strategy, formation and/or composition. For example, in Dartfish you can watch your fast break strategy and the software will tell you what the successful and unsuccessful parts were.

Coach feedback

Previous knowledge of your own and your opponent's strengths and weaknesses is valuable. Finding out the type of strategy, formation and/or composition that the opposition may apply could make the difference between winning and losing.

Personal reflection

Your personal evaluation of your own strengths and weaknesses and how they may affect the strategy, formation and/or composition is also key to your success.

'I am going to take every opportunity to smash the shuttle in my badminton game, as it's one of my key strengths.'

(GO!) Activity

Identify two methods you have used to gather information on your SFC. Complete the table below and say why these methods were useful in identifying strengths and weaknesses in your SFC. An example has been given for you.

Activity	Strategy, formation and/or composition	Method	Why useful
Netball	Centre pass strategy	Digital camera	I was able to play this image back time and time again to see where our centre pass strategy broke down.

Preparation for performance development

When preparing to develop your SFC you will need to consider some of the features mentioned previously:

- Individual and team strengths and weaknesses
- Opponent(s)' strengths and weaknesses
- Roles and responsibilities
- Performance conditions
- Strategy, formation and/or composition fundamentals

✔Assessment in PE

2.1 Describing strengths and areas for development in a performance or 'planning personal performance' in your portfolio.

Look at some of the examples on these pages and see how they might help you to plan the development of your SFC. You may have to consider adapting your SFC or perhaps you have decided to design specific practices to improve.

Approaches that impact positively on performance

It will be unlikely that you will use the same SFC throughout your performance or performances. Being able to adapt your SFC during your planning stages or during your performance will enable you to have approaches that can have a positive impact on you performance. There may be several reasons why you may have to adapt your SFC, for example:

- To exploit your opponent(s) weakness.

- To counteract a weakness of your own.

- The score or time in your performance.

- Your formation/composition does not make the most effective use of the choreographic devices.

Examples of the changes you may adopt

During your gymnastic performance you may have found that you have not used your floor patterns effectively. For example you may have too many straight-line patterns – adapting your floor patterns to include diagonal lines will have more of an impact on your performance.

In football, your opponents have been able to place a long ball over the top of your four defenders. By adapting your formation to add a sweeper at the back, you will be able to counteract this problem.

GO! Activity

After one of your performances, in a group review the outcome of the performance and any problems you encountered. Consider the following key questions:
- What was the problem?
- Why was it a problem?
- What was the impact on our performance?

For example, during a netball game, the goal attack was double marked, which led to the team being unable to successfully carry out its centre pass strategy.
Or
In a partner gymnastics formation/composition both performers were unable to keep in time with each other, resulting in a lack of coordinated movement, meaning the performance lacked fluidity.
Now consider how you might be able to adapt the SFC to find solutions to these problems. Consider the following key questions:

- What can we change?

- How do we apply this change?

- Will it result in a successful solution?

Here is a possible solution to the netball problem: the team could decide to use their wing defence to receive the initial pass, which would then link with their wing attack. This could give in a more positive result, where they would be able to create more space to allow for more passing options.

Here is a possible solution to the gymnastics problem: the performers could decide to reduce the amount of complicated movements in their routine so that they find it easier to coordinate their formation/composition, giving greater flow, with smoother links.

CfE focus

Working with others to devise a possible solution is giving you the opportunity to develop as a responsible citizen. Working in groups or in collaboration with others is a very important characteristic of citizenship within a successful society. If everyone feels their contribution is valued then confidence grows and people feel they have something to offer.

Practice sessions

Another approach to performance development is to consider practice sessions. You can plan practice sessions that will allow you to work on the parts of your SFC that are causing problems. You may wish to consider:

- Slowing the strategy down

- Walking through and talking through the strategy

- Unopposed practice

- Passive defenders

- Drawing out the formation

This will give you an opportunity to focus on refining your SFC. For example, during a fast break in basketball you may wish to work on the impact of this strategy through unopposed fast break drills. Some examples are given below.

Fast-break lay up drill

Purpose: to practise filling in positions on the fast break.

Procedure

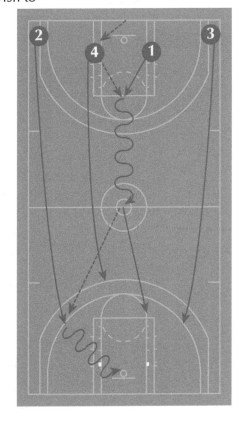

1. Four players participate in this drill, with no defenders. Players set up in front of the basket along the baseline: players 1 and 4 start at the blocks, players 2 and 3 start in the corners.

2. Player 4 tosses the ball off the backboard and rebounds. Player 1 cuts to the middle for an outlet pass, while players 2 and 3 run down the outside lanes for a pass at the opposite end.

3. Whoever receives the ball from player 1 takes the ball to the basket for a lay up; player 4 sprints down the court for a rebound.

4. Whether the shot is made or missed, player 4 grabs the ball and makes an outlet pass once again to player 1, and the fast break is executed on the other end.

Two-player fast break

Purpose: to practise passing and moving on the two-on-one fast break.

Procedure

1. Divide players into pairs – one pair will be on the court at a time. Place one defender at the opposite end of the floor.

2. The first pair of players runs down the floor, passing back and forth and trying to score on the other end against the defender.

3. After the pair scores or the defender stops them, the next two players go, and so on. Everyone attempts to score on the fast break against the defender.

4. After every pair has gone, switch defenders and ends, and change up pairs. The drill continues until everyone has played defence.

✔ Assessment in PE

1.3 Explaining two approaches to develop performance.

2.2 Preparing and implementing a personal development plan containing clearly identified development targets.

2.3 Selecting and applying two approaches to impact positively on a performance or 'planning, developing and implementing approaches to enhance personal performance' in your portfolio.

Look at some of the examples and see how they might help you to plan, develop and put into action approaches to help you improve your strategy, formation and/or composition. Now consider your own SFC. What plan of action have you considered to help you or your team improve the effectiveness of your SFC?

Check your progress

Complete the following to check your understanding.	HELP NEEDED	GETTING THERE	CONFIDENT
1. Name any strategy, formation and/or composition.	◯	◯	◯
2. What do you consider to be the main strategy, formation and/or composition factors that impact on your performance?	◯	◯	◯
3. How have you been able to gather information on these SFC factors?	◯	◯	◯
4. What approaches to development have you used?	◯	◯	◯
5. What impact have these approaches had on your performance and/or composition?	◯	◯	◯

Make a judgement – were you able to complete these easily? If not, go back and look over some of the explanations or speak to your teacher for further advice.

SECTION 2
The emotional factor

5 The emotional factor

This chapter deals with some of the emotional features that have an impact on your performance.

The features we are learning to identify are:

- Confidence
- Resilience
- Optimism
- Fear and anger

In this chapter you will learn:

1. How resilience, confidence, optimism, fear and anger can impact on performance.
2. How to gather information about these features.
3. How to prepare for performance development.
4. To understand and apply approaches to develop performance.
5. To monitor performance development.
6. To evaluate performance development.
7. To identify and explain future performance development needs.

🧠 What should I already know?

From your broad general education you will be familiar with some emotional features, as part of the health and wellbeing (HWB) experiences and outcomes (4–25a). You will also have some experience of observing your own and other's performance, to try to identify areas of strength and development needs (HWB 3/4–24a). Part of the work you will have done in class and perhaps in your own time will have been to try to improve the development needs. In the experiences and outcomes for HWB in your BGE you will have had to try to sustain fitness across all aspects (HWB 3–21a). You will also have recorded the progress you have made as you have worked and any improvements you have been able to see after training.

At National 4 and 5 you will take these skills and knowledge and use them in different activities to increase and deepen your learning about performance development.

What is the emotional factor?

There are a number of positive and negative emotions that impact on our ability to perform effectively. The main emotions are:

- Happiness

- Trust

- Surprise

- Fear

- Anger

Happiness and trust can be seen as positive emotions. Fear and anger are obviously negative and surprise is an emotion that can be both positive and negative.

These emotions influence qualities that are necessary for effective performance.

Emotion	Quality affected	Impact on performance
Happiness	Confidence	Willing to try, believe in own ability
	Resilience	Won't give up, will recover from losing or being beaten
	Optimism	Remaining positive and hopeful that success can be achieved
Trust	Self-respect	Conduct self in appropriate manner
	Mutual respect	Treat others with respect and courtesy
	Personal responsibility	Manage own emotions and behaviour
	Collective responsibility	Activity carried out without disagreements
Fear	Decision-making	Wrong or rash decisions are taken and hesitation occurs
	Confidence	Unwilling or unable to try, no belief in own ability
Anger	Decision-making	Wrong or rash decisions are taken and hesitation occurs
	Self-control	Wrong or rash decisions are taken, resulting in performer losing control

Let's look at three of the positive qualities that are influenced by happiness:

- Confidence

- Resilience

- Optimism

In sport and physical activity, good levels of confidence mean you can go on and perform in front of a large audience because you are sure your dance is of a high quality and you can feel confident you will remember everything you need to do. Good levels of confidence and the fact that you have rehearsed it many times in a familiar situation will give you belief in the ability of others in your group.

We will then look at the emotions of **fear** and **anger**.

:: Make the link

There are many circumstances in life where confidence is required. When you prepare well for an exam, you can allow yourself to feel hopeful you will pass it and achieve a good result. This means you have a positive outlook and in fact are said to have a positive mental state of mind. This will impact on your life in many ways. You will be able and willing to take on new challenges and will be encouraged by how you feel, even when dealing with circumstances that could be seen as negative. An optimistic person can usually see something positive in most circumstances. An optimistic person failing an exam would quite quickly be able to see that their preparation had perhaps been unfocused or inadequate and needed to be changed for the next attempt. Being optimistic encourages a good positive outlook.

Feature of the factor: Happiness — confidence

Having the correct amount of confidence will allow you to **feel** as though you are capable of performing well. This will allow you to cope with the emotions associated with **fear**. Confidence can allow you to begin a performance in the right state of mind. This means you are giving yourself the best possible chance of being successful right from the start.

A performer who has confidence is hopeful and positive of being able to believe things will go well. They are not afraid or frightened of the performance environment. This means they are optimistic. This enables them to concentrate on using the most effective skills and to make the right decisions at the right time.

Feature of the factor: Happiness — resilience

The emotion of happiness is also associated with resilience. Being resilient in sport means having the ability to recover from negative performances, from injury and even negative feedback. Athletes who manage to come back to training after a period of inactivity are said to be **resilient**. It means they are able to overcome circumstances and 'bounce back' to compete again. Often the emotion of fear, of further injury, pain or poor confidence levels affect a person's resilience.

A performer who is resilient is adaptable. In a performance situation this quality allows a dancer to get up from a bad landing and carry on to complete the performance. She would not be thrown or put off by the fact she landed on two feet instead of

🌑 Make the link

Resilience is often talked about in other subjects in school. In technology you will have worked with materials that have different **degrees** of resilience. Some metals when heated in science can go back to their original shape. In geography you will have looked at how resilient a rainforest is once it has been flattened then begins to re-grow. Communities are investigated in history that have been resilient and have recovered from war atrocities, famines or natural disasters.

Also, as part of your broad general PSHE programme you will have looked at different ways of coping and recovering when you get worried or upset about something.

one and would be able to adapt the next motif she had to do in her dance immediately. Being adaptable in any performance situation is a very positive characteristic. This allows you to 'think on your feet' and means you can cope with the unexpected – and most sporting and physical activities have unexpected elements.

GO! Activity

From the activities on your course create a Directory of Unexpected Occurrences – a list of things that can happen that are unplanned. This can be something that someone else does that influences your performance or changes the performance environment. Here is an example:

Activity: volleyball	Problem for me or my team	Possible course of action or adaptations for our team
Unexpected occurrence: The setter in the opposite team begins sending long high sets to the player in position 2 to spike from the very edge of the court.	Our two-man block is now dragged right out to the side to try to cope with this attack, leaving spaces near the middle of the court.	Encourage our third front court player to move towards the centre of the court, just off the net, to cover the exposed area.

How does resilience impact positively on performance

We often talk about adaptations we make to our tactics or to our choreographies. However performers need to be willing and able to apply these adaptations. It requires **resilience** to react to demands that change as the performance takes place. Being resilient means being confident enough to accept that we have to do something **other** than what we had originally planned to do.

Having resilient players on your team means that whatever the opposition do, it is likely that you will be able to respond well under pressure.

We can never plan or anticipate everything an opponent will do or everything that could go wrong during a performance. However, being resilient means we can rely on skills, experience and knowledge to help us cope and overcome new or unexpected challenges.

How does resilience impact negatively on performance

It is difficult to see any negative impact of resilience since this quality is only required in situations which do not go to plan.

Feature of the factor: Happiness — optimism

Happiness is an emotion that can make you feel optimistic. If you are happy you are more likely to be optimistic and if you are optimistic you are likely to be happier.

Optimism affects your confidence levels. Being optimistic allows us to have confidence and being confident means we are optimistic.

How does optimism impact positively on performance

Optimism in sports and physical activity means being able to hope for a good outcome. Winning or giving a good performance would be the good outcome. When you are optimistic it means another team or opponent does not intimidate you. Or as you go on to dance or perform a trampolining sequence, you can convince yourself that you are well prepared and ready to show what you can do. This means you have the best chance of success – so the impact of optimism is very positive.

How do these features impact negatively on performance?

By being too confident or optimistic it is possible that a performer could be too cocky and not treat opposition with the respect they deserve or prepare properly for the demands of an event, e.g. a dancer who has won a competition twice in a row might be over – confident that she will win again easily. As a result she might not rehearse enough or pay attention to more complex aspects of her performance. This might make the overall sequence messy and result in her dropping points.

Features of the factor: fear and anger

A certain amount of fear and anger are present in everyone. The ability to manage these emotions has a positive impact on performance.

How do fear and anger impact positively on performance?

Manageable amounts of fear make sure a performer is well prepared for the demands of an important event. Fear of failure can ensure that all training is completed to a high standard. Fear of this kind can also encourage a performer to try hard and not give up.

Managed anger too, in the correct measure, gives a performer a certain degree of determination. This means that in a challenge the right amount of drive and commitment would be present, meaning a tackle would be firm and lack any hesitation. The emotion of anger can be 'channelled' positively. By managing anger a performer can be more assertive. This means they carry out their duties with confidence and commitment, e.g. a defender in a tight situation will not make a rushed, rash tackle when under pressure after being beaten to the ball.

Anger can only be used effectively if it is channelled correctly.

How do fear and anger impact negatively on performance?

The negative emotions of fear and anger are very closely linked. Fear means feeling frightened as a result of some sort of danger.

This can make a person panic and do something unexpected or react unreasonably or irrationally.

This means the person might not even have time to think and may instinctively say or do something they might not otherwise do.

In a performance situation fear of failure might make a performer lose confidence in their ability and make them feel nervous and pessimistic (the opposite of optimistic).

In sprint events, fear of losing might affect nerves and then make a runner react too quickly to the starter's gun – in fact moving a fraction of a second before the starter's gun goes off – causing a false start.

Panic can also come about as a result of **fear** – making you respond by doing the **wrong** thing. Panic means you have no time to think or to measure up what response you **should** make. This leads to **confusion** – another negative impact of fear.

Therefore, in a performance situation, fear and anger can make your decision-making inconsistent.

These emotions might also result in a performer hesitating to tackle a player dribbling up the wing in hockey, in case they do not win the tackle or miss the ball and hit the player, perhaps risking a second yellow card, thereby being sent off.

Making rash tackles on players about to score is often the outcome of fear. The player on the receiving end of the rash tackle might respond in anger, illustrating how these negative emotions can often make an unwanted appearance in sport. Anger again makes performers react – often instinctively. This means they lose self-control. This can have serious effects in a performance situation.

In rugby, fear of being hurt could stop a smaller hooker moving to tackle a bigger, stronger-looking player in possession of the ball running forwards about to score a try.

Managing these emotions forms part of the training top-level players do. Psychologists are employed by many big football clubs to help their temperamental, emotionally charged, top-level players keep control of these emotions so that they can stay on the pitch and do their jobs.

Similarly, it is well known that some managers and coaches exploit the emotional states of the opposition in order to effect an individual's play.

It is wise to remember that the **amounts** of these qualities should be a consideration when performing. Too high a level of fear, anger, confidence or optimism could have a negative impact on performance.

GO! Activity

Research a number of different activities to find personalities in the world of sport, dance and gymnastics who are affected by poor management of their emotions. Make a poster of the activities, names and problems these performers have.

GO! Activity

Make a mind map of one of these qualities and show that you understand how performance might be affected in an activity of your choice. Here is an example:

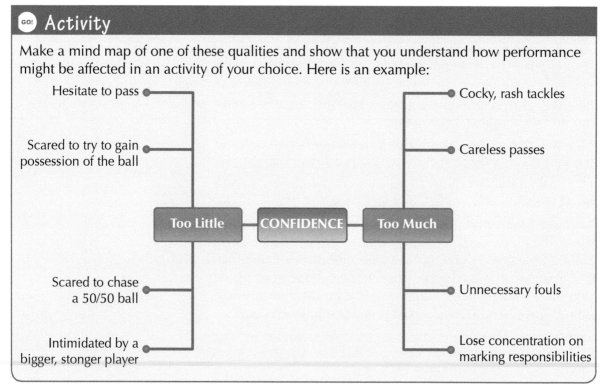

Hesitate to pass

Scared to try to gain possession of the ball

Scared to chase a 50/50 ball

Intimidated by a bigger, stonger player

Too Little — **CONFIDENCE** — **Too Much**

Cocky, rash tackles

Careless passes

Unnecessary fouls

Lose concentration on marking responsibilities

🌳 Skills for life, learning and work

Management of our emotions in the world of work means we are more likely to be good leaders and are able to work effectively in teams or groups.

By understanding our own emotions we can make sense of why we feel what we feel and, more importantly, what needs to be done with these feelings so that we can proceed throughout our lives in a positive, successful manner.

For example, when speaking to someone on the phone who begins to get angry, a person who can manage their own emotions will be able to bring the conversation to a satisfactory outcome. It makes sense to say that if we can manage our own emotions then fear, confusion and panic cannot affect us. This means that in any situation, the choice of action we take is more likely to be appropriate.

💎 CfE focus

All of these qualities are a major focus for the new curriculum. By encouraging these positive emotional characteristics it is very likely that **effective contributors, responsible citizens, successful learners** and **confident individuals** will be the end product. Every citizen will feel like they have a part to play in society and will have the emotional wellbeing that enables them to cope with the ever-changing demands of their own lives.

☑ Assessment in PE

1.2 Explaining in detail the impact of one positive and one negative factor on performance.

You may wish to use some of the information about the emotions mentioned in this section that can have an effect on performance. It is also useful when completing your portfolio to show that you understand the emotional factors that can influence your performance.

How do I gather information on emotional factors?

Using a checklist is a good way to gather information on how you feel before, during and after performances. A checklist might ask you to **rate** how confident you feel, how nervous you feel or how optimistic or pessimistic you feel. Another, more straightforward way for you to collect data is to use a 'personal reflections diary' and to complete it before and after the activity you are investigating.

Here is a possible layout for a personal reflections diary.

Activity: swimming

Date	Feelings before the event	Feelings during the event	Feelings after the event	I think I need to try to…
18 May	I feel quite nervous and that I will never be able to win. I think all the other girls are better than me, stronger and fitter and even more confident.	I couldn't shut out the feelings of nervousness as I stood on the block waiting to dive. My legs were wobbly and I felt sick. Once in the water I forgot my plan to focus on my breathing rhythm and instead I tried to keep up with the swimmer in the next lane to me.	I felt quite positive as I came fourth and I beat the girl who I had watched at the beginning of the race who I thought was much better and stronger than me. I was angry with myself for not getting into my stoke pattern quicker as I could now see that when I did some of the feelings of doubt and panic disappeared.	Not watch the others warm up. Get into my stoke pattern quickly.

GO! Activity

Make up a personal reflections diary for your own activity.

Try to be as honest as you can about how you feel so that you are able to gather evidence which will be useful to you when you begin to investigate the impact of these emotions on your performance. You should add a column to your diary for an observer to contribute any comments about changes in your behaviour or your technique they witnessed while you performed. By linking together your own feelings and reflections, along with information from the observer, you should be able to gather data about how your behaviour and your technique were affected by your emotional state.

For example, in swimming, if the coach was able to tell you that, as you began to establish your breathing pattern as the race progressed, you began to fight back into fifth, then fourth place, you would be able to reflect that this was the point in the race where you felt calmer or were less distracted by the swimmers around you. The feedback from your coach, combined with your own reflections, would confirm that when you took control of your emotions you were able to perform better.

✔ Assessment in PE

3.1 Seeking feedback from others.
For this assessment standard you could put the information given by your coach in your personal reflections diary to help you plan the next steps in your development programme.

Appropriateness of methods of data collection

This is a useful way to gather information about how emotions can impact on you positively and negatively while you perform. As this data collection is about your own honest reflections about how you felt, it is likely to be very personal and useful to you. By having a coach or observer watch the same performance, your own reflections can be corroborated – backed up – by another set of observation data. This makes the results more reliable and valid. It is also useful, as with any performance observations, to film the performance and then use the slow motion, rewind and pause facilities this gives you to help make sure your reflections are accurate. Often the effects of how you are feeling can be seen in the way you dance, play or swim. It is possible to match up your personal reflections with what you see on your filmed recordings.

🔵 Activity

Film your performance and try to note any examples of when fear, confidence, optimism or anger had an impact on your performance. Use the following questions to guide you.

- Can you see when you perhaps panicked?
- What happened to your performance when this panic took over?
- Are there any signs of anger?
- How did the anger impact on the performance?

Record these observations in a personal reflections diary.

☑Assessment in PE

2.1 Describing strengths and areas for development in performance.

Some of the methods given in this section might be useful for you to use to identify areas of your own performance that are strengths and development needs.

In your portfolio you will also need to give information about the monitoring, recording and evaluation of performance development. This section of the book can help you do that.

∴ Make the link

Part of your course assessment includes a one-off performance where you have to demonstrate effective management of your emotions while you perform. By being knowledgeable about what emotions affect your performance, you should be able to minimise the negative effects they might have.

Preparation for performance development

Improving performance through increased awareness of emotions is quite a challenging and long-term process. However, for the performer who lacks confidence or who finds it difficult to keep control of their temper when they get angry during a performance, it is a very worthwhile process. The process you go through will be totally personal to you and will involve you examining how you feel, what impact these feelings have on your performance and following through a personal programme of work before and after you perform. It can take some time to improve these emotional areas, but it is very likely that if you persevere it will have a major positive impact on your overall performance. Bear this in mind as you train – the results will be worth it! You must be clear about which emotions are causing you the most problems. This will allow you to set yourself targets for improvement.

GO! Activity

Look at your personal reflections diary. Is there an emotion that has a negative impact on your performance? Is there more than one emotion that makes your performance less successful than it should be? Is this something you feel you want to try to tackle? If the answer is yes, then complete the following graphic organiser.

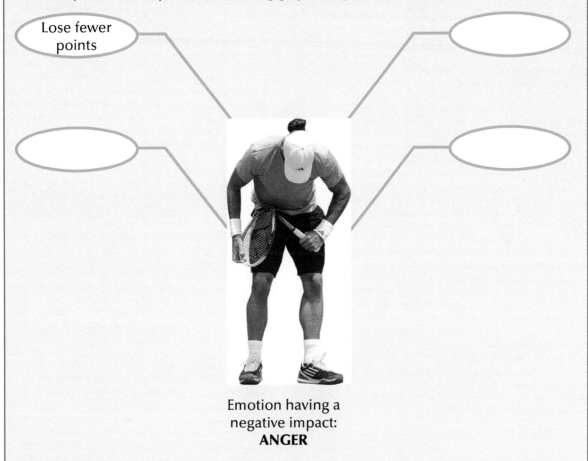

Lose fewer points

Emotion having a
negative impact:
ANGER

Copy this graphic organiser and identify in the outside boxes what the performance would look like if this emotion were to be managed more effectively.

Now go through this same process for your chosen activity. Your target is to reduce the influence of your most negative emotion in your performance.

✔ Assessment in PE

2.1 Describing strengths and areas for development in a performance.

By using these methods to identify which of the emotions affect your performance both positively and negatively you can achieve this standard. You would need to describe the problems these emotions cause you or the benefits you get from being able to use them effectively when performing.

Approaches that impact positively on performance

Both of the negative emotions of fear and anger we have been looking at can be improved by using similar types of training. This training can improve decision-making, confidence and self-control qualities. By identifying what it is that triggers a loss of control of the emotions, you can organise and prepare for what you **should** do in a 'trigger' situation. In this way anger and fear can be controlled to some extent.

🔘 Activity

Look back at the film of your performance and your personal reflections diary. Can you identify the trigger that makes you start to lose control? This could be something another player does, something the audience does, something an official does or something you do yourself, e.g. put a serve out of court. List them in a 'triggers' table. For example:

Activity: badminton

Emotion identified: anger	Impact on performance	Trigger
E.g. I threw my racquet on the ground.	I lost the point and the umpire warned me about un-sportsmanlike behaviour.	I had just lost three serves in a row.

Approaches to dealing with triggers

Describe and identify as many triggers as possible that make you lose focus on your performance. Then identify any **common** triggers. Are they things that **you** do or things that **someone else** does? If your performance is mainly affected by your reactions to something you do, then you must deliberately plan a new response to these situations.

Developing skills to identify **when** things start to go wrong, and then deliberately making sure the response to these situations is appropriate, is a worthwhile intention to help manage anger or fear. This establishes the link between 'triggers and responses.'

Training for minimising the impact of these negative emotions should begin within class practice sessions. Dealing with 'triggers' in a less competitive/demanding environment allows you to get more experience identifying changes in the way you feel. It also allows you to have a little more time to try to compose yourself and put in place your new 'response'.

Approach 1: deep breathing

Deep breathing is a recognised approach to help manage anger and fear. Lots of practice in less competitive/less challenging environments will be required in order for this approach to help. The technique of filling the lungs completely then releasing the air very slowly while concentrating on controlling the breathing muscles is an excellent way to change the focus from what just went wrong to bring the mind back under control. This type of training should be included at the beginning of each training session to make sure the performer is able to carry out the approach properly. This clears the mind of mistakes and allows appropriate decisions to be made.

For example, the new response to losing three serves in a row in badminton would be to take three **deep breaths** while looking at your racquet head. To then look up and be ready to receive the serve from your opponent. It sounds simple, but trying to put in place a new response to the frustration of feeling that you are not in control is a challenge.

The theory is that, as you begin to be able to see and feel these triggers in practice or training sessions you can, in a more competitive or challenging situation, quickly and effectively respond in an appropriate rehearsed manner. This will almost certainly have a positive impact on your own performance and, interestingly, upon your opponent too.

Approach 2: visualisation

If your emotions are triggered as a result of something **someone else** does then you should undertake training that involves shutting out distractions and focusing on the requirements of the performance. This will make sure that your confidence remains high. This is an approach called **visualisation**. Again in class practice sessions before the performance begins you should find a quiet place to sit and prepare for the demands of performance. You should run through the beginning of the performance, deliberately focusing on where you have to go, when you have to start and how the performance begins. A gymnast, trampolinist, swimmer or dancer should visualise themselves carrying out their sequences perfectly in front of the audience. They should run over this in their minds many times, shutting out the noise of the crowd or the presence of other competitors. This process of seeing yourself as being successful encourages confidence and reduces the impact of fear or of losing control.

For a games player, the conditions of where you will play should be something you try to see a picture of in your 'mind's eye'. This will help you begin to focus from the first few minutes of play. Then repeat in your head the plan you have for the performance. This might include what type of serve you will begin using, where you will stand to receive service, who your opponent is, what hand they dribble with or where you must position yourself in defence and attack. It is vital that only a few **key** areas are focused on at this point, otherwise panic and confusion might take over as you try to remember everything involved in the performance. By using this visualisation approach you can prepare well in advance of the performance beginning. This means you will be calm and ready to begin with your emotions under control. You are more likely to be able to judge what needs to be done, making good decisions and managing the emotions that come to the surface while performing.

Approach 3: mental rehearsal

It is useful to rehearse in your head what you will do if any of the triggers you have identified happen in the performance. This is identical to the training mentioned before. This **mental rehearsal approach** encourages you to run over set responses to some situations. For example, you will remember how you feel when you step up to take a free throw. By using the mental rehearsal approach you can practise in your mind the routines you could follow before, during and after taking the shot. In practice you can tell yourself to feel confident, to encourage yourself to use your excellent technique so that when you go onto court in a match, you will have prepared yourself to manage your emotions.

Approach 4: positive self-talk

The positive self-talk approach can be used to help manage anger or fear. To do this you must develop **alternate** positive responses to negative triggers. This could be saying key words to yourself or repeating a phrase designed to help you stay in control when tackled badly, for example, or when in a stressful situation such as the free throw mentioned above. By having a pre-rehearsed phrase to say as you step up to shoot, the effects of fear can be significantly reduced. For example, saying 'Look, aim, score' can increase confidence and distractions can be shut out.

By practising these new responses in training situations they will become more automatic and result in you being able to keep control throughout the performance.

You need to practise in training what you **should** do if your emotions are triggered to make you feel angry. Basketball players who miss three point-shooting opportunities often use the 'park it' phrase. This is used constantly in training to try to get the players used to moving on from mistakes they make and to keep anger and frustration at bay.

Only by trying time after time to replace negative responses to negative emotions with positive self-talk will you be able to manage your emotions in a 'live' performance situation.

✔Assessment in PE

2.3 Selecting and applying two approaches to impact positively on a performance.

The approaches described in this section could be used to help you carry out a programme of work to help you improve your performance.

Monitoring and evaluating

The monitoring of training completed should continue in your personal reflections diary. This should record how you felt before, during and after performances. It must also include reflections on how your training is progressing. This will allow you to change your approach if necessary.

The evaluation of how effective your training has been in impacting on performance should be a straightforward comparison of the personal reflections diary gathered before you started training and the one completed after training. If there are fewer incidents of you losing control of your temper, or feeling less frightened, or more evidence of increased confidence, then your training has had a positive impact on your overall performance. Your discipline record might also give you evidence of the progress you have made while working on these emotions.

Make the link

In the skill development part of the course you will have learned about the stages of learning. With emotional performance development we are trying to replace responses that have become automatic, as you might have used them for a long time. We have to use more appropriate and acceptable responses again and again before they become automatic, positive responses to a stressful performance situation.

☑ Assessment in PE

2.4 Monitoring and recording performance development sessions.

By using the personal reflections diary you can provide evidence of how you monitored the work you carried out.

3.2 Evaluating the effectiveness of the personal development plan in supporting performance development.

3.3 Evaluating progress based on all information gathered.

By comparing the results in your personal reflections diary you could evaluate how successful the programme of work has been in helping you to manage your emotions.

Future needs

This is an area a performer must keep a very close eye on. Sometimes the physical preparation for performance is the focus and we forget that when our emotions make us lose control then we cannot possibly be giving our best performance. Future considerations would ensure that a performer continues to be aware of his or her emotions and begins to consider an opponent's emotional state – in order to exploit it and/or to gain confidence.

Check your progress

Complete the following to check your understanding.	HELP NEEDED	GETTING THERE	CONFIDENT
1. Choose one emotion and explain how it impacts on your performance positively.	◯	◯	◯
2. Choose one emotion and explain how it impacts on your performance negatively.	◯	◯	◯
3. Describe how you would gather information on the emotional factor.	◯	◯	◯
4. Describe the process you went through to improve any quality affected by an emotion.	◯	◯	◯
5. Explain what future needs you might have in terms of the emotional factor.	◯	◯	◯

Make a judgement – were you able to complete these easily? If not, go back and look over some of the explanations or speak to your teacher for further advice.

SECTION 3
The mental factor

6 The mental factor

This chapter deals with the mental fitness features that have an impact on your performance.

The features we are learning to identify and develop are:

- Level of arousal
- Concentration
- Decision-making

In this chapter you will learn:

1. How these features can impact on performance.
2. How to gather information about these features.
3. How to prepare for performance development.
4. To understand and apply approaches to develop performance.
5. To monitor performance development.
6. To evaluate performance development.
7. To identify and explain future performance development needs.

🧠 What should I already know?

From your broad general education you will have become familiar with many of these features of mental fitness. This was part of the health and wellbeing (HWB) experiences and outcomes (4–25a). You will also have some experience observing your own and others performance to identify areas of strength and development needs (HWB 3/4–24a). Part of the work you have done in class and perhaps in your own time will have been to try to improve the development needs. In the experiences and outcomes for HWB in your BGE you will have had to sustain fitness across all aspects (HWB 3–21a). You will also have recorded your progress and any improvements you were able to see after training.

At National 4 and 5 you will take these skills and knowledge and use them in different activities to increase and deepen your learning about performance development.

Feature of the factor: level of arousal

All mental features are associated with a cognitive process within the brain. This means there is some sort of deliberate thinking involved.

Level of arousal relates to your attitude about performing – if you are 'up for it' or not.

Before you go on to perform, you should be aware of how ready you are to begin the performance.

How does this feature impact positively on your performance?

When your level of arousal is at the right level you are prepared to give your best, to shut out any distractions and to carry out whatever decisions you need to make right from the beginning of the performance. This means you are likely to do well.

Getting the level of arousal right means you have the chance to concentrate on the important parts of your performance quickly and settle into giving a successful display of the skills you have.

How does this feature impact negatively on your performance?

If a performer has too high a level of arousal then they could go on to play and find that they make rash decisions, resulting in them fouling another player just because they are too keen to do well. This could result in them being booked or even sent off.

In tennis, low levels of arousal might come about because of the result of a previous match against the same opponent. If a player has been beaten significantly before, then it is likely that the performer would not want to play this person again for fear of losing badly for the second time. This would mean they would go into the match doubting their own ability, wanting the match to be over quickly, possibly not trying as hard as they could and even giving up early on in the match. In a creative activity the performer with a low level of arousal will be less motivated to compete and might not try as hard as they should.

How do I gather information on this feature?

Features within the mental factor are very difficult to measure and gather evidence about. This is because the observations are usually opinions (known as subjective observations). You need to try to gather evidence with only some opinion and provide some factual observations to back up these opinions.

GO! Activity

Complete the table in discussion with a partner or a group. Discuss which statements are facts and which are opinions.

Aspect of performance	Fact	Opinion
The score is 3–2		
The gymnast performed a round-off		
The goal attack scored the last goal		
The round-off the gymnast performed was effective		
The swimmer's time was 45 seconds		
The swimmer's arm action is correct		
***		
***		

Decide on one more feature of performance that you agree is a fact and one that you agree is opinion. Insert these in your table in the bottom two rows at ***.

Although the facts we gather about a performance are very important, your own opinions are good indicators about how you feel a performance went – as long as you are honest.

Other opinions can come from a coach or teacher. These people are generally knowledgeable and experienced about the activities they deliver. Therefore, in this factor, the information they generate can provide vital details about how a performance looks or how the performer behaves. When put together with some more factual evidence from observation analysis, the picture they provide can be very useful.

Think about other observation schedules you have used in other areas of the course. You might consider adding a section to gather information relating to the impact of the level of arousal on your performance.

Here is an example of the information you could add to your GOS.

Level of arousal		
Before the match	During the match	After the match

Another way to gather information is through coach feedback. This can highlight the body language you demonstrate when your level of arousal drops. By adding a space on your general observation schedule related to how 'up for it' you were before the performance started, judgements can be made about your level of arousal as the performance progresses.

For example, if before you went on to play in an important basketball match you felt down, overwhelmed and negative with a fear of losing, it's possible to say you didn't begin the match in the correct frame of mind to do well. This might be displayed in the way you walked onto court, nervously and uncertain, or even how much you contributed during the pre-match chat with your teammates.

Another example might be a dancer being observed fidgeting nervously as she waited for her cue to go on stage.

Personal reflections diary

By keeping a personal reflections diary it would be possible to record feelings before, during and after a performance. The diary would allow you to gather information about how you felt throughout a variety of different performances. You might, for example, be able to identify that it is only when people you know are in the audience that you feel particularly stressed or doubt your ability.

By identifying the different circumstances and environments in which your performance takes place you will be able to begin to link these to how you feel about going on to perform.

The diary might have the following types of headings:

Type of competition	Venue	Date	Audience	Observations about my level of arousal before and during performance
Inter-club match	Longridge sports centre	21 April	Only parents and friends – no members of the public	Felt quite keen to get on and play. Got on court quickly and started warming-up. I knew most of the people who were playing in my age group. Lost a few points in a row at service but always felt I would pull it back. Fought hard and went on to win the match.
District badminton tournament	The Deans centre	25 April	Parents, friends and selectors for Scottish squad	Very nervous, felt sick, didn't want to play. Waited for opponent to offer to begin warm-up instead of getting on court right away Made many errors early on and saw the selectors walk away, felt like giving up, that I'd blown my chances of showing them how good I was.

Feature of the factor: concentration

Concentration is your brain's ability to focus on what is going on within a performance situation. The brain is able to use all your body's senses to pick up information about what has to be done.

How does this feature impact positively on your performance?

A brain that is trained to concentrate can shut out distractions that are unimportant and stay focused on what it is you have to do.

Good **concentration** allows you to direct your focus on, for example, who you have to mark, where the ball should be played, where the 'take off' line is, when to begin to move. Your mind chooses not to dwell on things which might distract it from what has to be done.

A performer who is concentrating is often said to be 'in the zone', making fewer mistakes, staying calm when under pressure, able to **solve problems** easily and generally in control of their performance.

How does this feature impact negatively on your performance?

A performer who is unable to concentrate will:

- find it difficult to stay with an opponent
- be affected by a crowd supporting the opposition
- find it difficult to carry out role-related duties within a team.
- be unable to cope well with any mistakes made while performing.

This means that the performance will suffer.

Another example might be a dancer who is feeling there is too much to remember in her dance routine. She might fail to concentrate on where her partner is in the dance and miss her cue to perform a jump together. This would make the dance look messy and disorganised.

GO! Activity

Look at these pictures. Use them to help you make a mind map showing how a performer's concentration might affect performance.

How do I gather information on this feature?

In a hockey general observation schedule the following row might be added to find out how concentration levels change throughout the game.

	Yes	No
Marks opponent appropriately for the entire match		

The personal reflections diary used earlier for the level of arousal feature is also a good way of gathering information about your concentration during a performance. By using a video of your performance it would be useful to reflect on particular parts of the performance where you lost concentration. This might show itself in different ways.

For example, you might not have been aware that the wind had changed direction while the golf competition had progressed. It is possible you would then play the wrong shot.

In a handball match you might not have noticed one of the opposition team signalling for a quick pass up court to enable her to catch the ball just as she arrived at the edge of the shooting circle. By looking at the video footage, your lack of concentration might be easy to see.

A performer often knows when she loses concentration. It could be after a very tiring rally or after four or five points are lost in a row. Instead of focusing on the game plan, concentration can be diverted to thoughts about the game being over, the championship lost or the disappointment supporters are going to experience as they watch the match being lost.

A personal reflections diary focusing on concentration might be a useful mechanism to record these observations.

You might have the following headings:

Date	Time	Event	Errors I made	Was this a result of poor concentration?
26 July	8pm	School ski slalom competition	I missed the fourth pole in the run as I almost fell coming out of the third and I forgot I needed to dig my edges in as I went round the fourth.	Yes
25 Feb	11.45	Inter-class volleyball match	I was concentrating on the opposition's setter and did not notice the back court hitter coming forward ready to attack. This meant we moved to the wrong area of the court to set the block.	Yes

Activity

For an activity of your choice identify where poor concentration could affect your overall performance. Add it to this table:

Activity	Scenario	Result
Football	Poor concentration means a player might not be marking his opponent.	A player from the opposite team is running behind the defender about to receive a pass.
Netball	Poor concentration means the wing attack has her back to her opponent and is only watching the ball.	She does not see the wing defence signal for a pass over the wing attack's head into the space.
Basketball	Poor concentration means the guard does not see the screen being set.	The opposition have a clear run in for a successful lay up.
Dance	Poor concentration means in a pair one dancer is unaware that she is out of time with her partner.	The dance looks messy and the dancers are out of time with each other.
Trampolining	Poor concentration means the performer does not stay in the middle of the bed.	He loses points for his overall sequence.

Feature of the factor: decision-making

By being able to make decisions early, we learn to 'read' a situation, establish which things are unimportant, less important and very important. This helps us anticipate what **might** happen and we can begin to think ahead to plan our possible course of action.

Decision-making in a performance environment means making use of:

- Our senses (sight, hearing and kinaesthetic)
- Our past experience
- Our ability to 'read' what needs to be done

How does this feature impact positively on your performance?

By being able to do the right thing at the right time we are more likely to be successful. When we see a player preparing to jump to spike, we need to decide when to jump to block, where to position our arms and how to land safely.

This ability to make decisions quickly and effectively allows us to **solve** performance **problems**. Again problem-solving is dependent on what our senses 'read' needs to be done and whether we have faced this situation before. Our brains are skilled at finding the correct response and so making the correct decision to deal with a specific problem if it has had to deal with this problem before.

A skilled goalkeeper is able to react quickly to decide to dive to the correct side because he has seen where the ball is going. This solves the problem of stopping the ball going in the net. In the gymnastics vault there are lots of decisions to be made and problems which have to be solved instantly, e.g. where to begin the run-up from, how fast to run, where to position the hands on the box, when to tuck the body in, when to open out, how to land, how to balance on landing and how to stop stepping forwards.

The brain with practice can decide how to 'solve these problems' and help produce a successful performance.

How does this feature impact negatively on your performance?

Poor decision-making means you are unlikely to be able to solve performance problems. When in a 'live' performance situation you are likely to make mistakes and to find it difficult to take advantage of an opponent. You might miss clues as to what the opponent might do next. This means you can't anticipate their play or possibly even exploit their weaknesses. For example, by passing the ball to the person who has a defender marking them closely instead of the other teammate who has some space to run into, possession could be given away and your team put under pressure. Again, this is a result of making a decision which is incorrect.

The ability to make the correct decision about who to pass to in a game can be the difference between winning and losing. Skilled players who have the ability to make an accurate pass almost instinctively are likely to be very valuable players in a team.

How do I gather information on this feature?

In badminton you might consider the decision-making abilities a player demonstrates when under pressure by counting how many times he plays the shuttle away from an opponent. This could indicate that he is able to observe where the player is standing and also, more importantly, make the right decision about what he should do next.

	Never	Sometimes	Always
Plays the shuttle away from opponent			

✔ Assessment in PE

2.1 Describing strengths and areas for development in a performance.

These mental features all affect your ability to do the right thing at the right time. By describing their influence on your performance you will achieve this assessment standard.

Appropriateness of methods of data collection

The methods you use to gather information about the mental factor must allow you to go back and re-use them so that you can measure any improvement after training.

You should try to record your performances to allow you to complete any observation accurately. This of course gives you the facility to pause while you read your observation schedule, or to rewind to check you have ticked the correct box.

You might even get a teacher or coach to confirm the assessments you are making.

This makes your observations more reliable and will provide a sound foundation to base any training decisions upon.

appropriate level of arousal + concentration = effective decision making

These features are linked together.

With the right **level of arousal**, the mind is able to **concentrate** on the right **decisions** to make in order to solve any performance problems which arise.

Skills for life, learning and work

In the world of work, employers are looking for their workers to **want** to do their best – have a good level of arousal for the job they must do. This means they are more likely to be able to listen and follow instructions properly (to be able to **concentrate**) and to make the right **decisions** and solve their own problems effectively when left to work unsupervised.

☆ CFE focus

These features can all impact on the success you achieve in your learning. If you are unaware of the impact of these mental factors on your decision-making, your commitment to learning and the ability you have to solve problems for yourself, then it will be more difficult for you to achieve all you are capable of. Understanding what these features are, what impact they have on you and, most importantly, how you can manage them, will enable you to become a successful learner.

☑ Assessment in PE

1.1 Explaining in detail two methods used to identify factors impacting on performance.

Although these methods include some **opinion** about the factor that is influencing decision making, when joined together with a personal reflections diary they can provide an accurate record of level of arousal, concentration and decision-making skills.

For example, when using the badminton example above to gauge the number of times the player decides to play the shuttle away from their opponent, a personal reflections diary would confirm if the player was aware of where the opponent was actually standing. Including these details in an explanation would ensure you achieve the assessment standard.

⦂ Make the link

The approaches available to improve levels of arousal and concentration are very similar. In fact, the approaches you would use to work on **all** of the features within the mental factor will be very similar to those approaches you would use when developing the emotional factor.

Preparation for performance development

Mental fitness is a requirement for every activity. When preparing to improve any of the features described it would be wise to understand that any approaches used will probably be for the long term. That is, you will probably include mental preparation before every performance. In this way your level of arousal, concentration and decision-making will have been considered before you go on to dance, swim or play.

The same methods can be used to improve levels of arousal or concentration.

Approach 1: deep breathing

Deep breathing has been used in many different walks of life to help people focus and shut out unnecessary distractions.

The method is only really possible when you are in a situation where you can stop, pause and take the deep breaths which allow you to control your rate of breathing and enable you to focus your concentration on whatever you have to do.

Deep breathing is particularly effective if a performer suffers from anxiety, and can be used before the performance begins to settle feelings of nervousness and allow concentration on the aspect of performance needing immediate attention. This method is also helpful in controlling your level of arousal. It helps you shut out feelings of self-doubt and allows you to take control of feelings which might mean you don't want to go on to perform. Deep breathing can also help when a performer's level of arousal is too high. For example, it can help bring into line heightened or increased levels of confidence, aggression and enthusiasm.

- Begin by closing your eyes and taking in a series of deep breaths, controlling how slowly you breathe the air in and how slowly you blow the air out.
- The breathing in is done slowly. Focus on getting as much air into the lungs as possible. Just before breathing

out, hold the breath for a second and then slowly and gently blow the air back out.

- While doing this, focus on the feeling of the air filling your chest and try to block out any noise or other distractions around you. In this way you are clearing your mind, ready to focus on whatever the performance problem might be.

- Try to focus on the rhythm of the breathing pattern and **not** on how you feel, who is watching or, for example, what the score was the last time you did this vault.

- Do this for at least five minutes before you go on to perform, or for as long as it takes you to get control of your breathing, leaving you feeling calm and in control.

As you become skilled at managing this aspect of your performance it is likely you will continue to use deep breathing as part of your warm-up and preparation for any event. Your level of arousal and concentration before you begin will most likely improve. This gives you the best chance possible to make effective decisions during your performance.

Approach 2: imagery and mental rehearsal

Imagery and mental rehearsal are both methods that allow a performer to visualise the correct pattern of movements or set sequences before they have to be performed. This can help control their level of arousal and make their mind concentrate on what will be involved in the performance and the decisions they are about to make.

A team of rowers mentally rehearsing their performance before a race

These techniques can be used at the beginning of a performance to prepare the mind for the challenges which lie ahead, to reinforce the responsibilities a performer has and to rehearse the kind of responses/decisions a performer may need to make during a performance.

The performer would find a quiet place to think through in their head the areas of the performance they need to focus on. This might be parts of the performance that are particularly challenging or areas where a great deal of concentration and focus are required.

The performer would then play through in their mind a series of pictures showing them making the correct decisions and being in control of the performance situation – being one step ahead, in effect. The image would always be one in which the performance was successful. This sequence would be repeated over and over in the performer's mind – rehearsed just like a speech you might give in drama until it was very familiar.

Prior to every performance, the performer will spend a little more time preparing mentally for what lies ahead, adding any new situations (images) that require consideration, pre-planning or in effect **rehearsal**. The successful sequence would be rehearsed many times within the brain so that it could be recalled when necessary in the 'live' performance.

A rugby player will use imagery before taking the conversion kick. He stops, waits and runs through the sequence of movements in his mind. Only when he has seen it successfully in his mind will he take the kick.

Approaches to develop decision-making

Approach 1: graphic organiser approach

This method makes you assess the environment in which you are performing and the problems and solutions you might need to consider. Really, this just means identifying the important decisions you need to make and all of the problems you might come across.

You must identify the **p**roblems and the **o**ptions which are available to you and the **o**utcomes you would achieve by **ch**oosing these options (POOCH analysis).

Problem	Option	Outcome	Choice
What problems can you see in your performance that need solving?	What are the possible solutions I could use?	What will happen if I decide to follow this course of action?	Which option will I choose to use in the performance.
E.g. My opponent is making me chase the shuttle around the court as she has a wide variety of strokes available to her which are strong.	• I could try to move her from side to side of the court.	She would have to use her backhand which I can see is her weakest stroke of all.	I will try to force her to the back of the court as often as possible as, even though her backhand is weak, I might be inaccurate in my attempts to play it there.
	• I could try to disguise what stroke I am going to play.	She would be wrong footed and I might be able to take back some control of the game.	I find disguising my shots difficult and so might make mistakes trying to do this.
	• I could try and force her to the back of the court and wait for a space to play the shuttle into.	She might get tired and then I could take advantage and make her move away from the base position more often until I found the space to play the shuttle into.	I decide to force her to the back of the court and put pressure on her to stay there. When she does I will attempt a drop shot.

In your lessons your teacher might ask you to examine parts of your performance.

You will have to want to improve (have the appropriate level of arousal) and be able to concentrate on what has to be done.

In badminton she might instruct your training buddy to keep you at the back of the court for as long as is possible, then stop the game and ask you:

- Can you Identify what was going on?
- What problems did you face? (Problems)
- What options did you try to overcome these problems? (Options and choices)
- Which of these things were successful?

In this way you will begin to learn which options match the problems you come across and then become more familiar with the decisions which you have to make to be successful.

> Problem A + Option B = Success

It would be useful after finishing to take note in a training or personal reflections diary of the aspects of the performance that were challenging and the steps you took to try to overcome these problems. By identifying aspects of the performance for which you had **no** options or problems you could **not** solve you can make a start at looking at the kind of decisions you have difficulty with.

This would help you to start to become familiar with the problem and to identify and try out possible options or solutions.

When you set up the same kind of problem in a practice session you can slowly, with support, decide what you could do to try to help you overcome this problem the **next time** you were faced with it. This helps the brain become familiar with lots of performance problems and decide their matching options or solutions.

This builds up an armoury of responses to performance 'situations'. By using this approach you will become increasingly aware of times during performance where you have successfully made the correct decision, choosing the correct option to solve the problem.

The theory is that the more you face these problems in practice and then make use of them in a 'live' performance situation, the more likely it is that you will be able to respond with the correct decision each time you need to.

Approach 2: the 'performance problem' scenarios approach

This approach to improving decision-making gradually builds up the **number** of decisions to be made and the **speed** at which these decisions have to be made.

 Fact

Armoury – in this context this word means a 'stock of resources' for you to use when performing.

For example, to improve the smash in tennis you would begin with a simple shadowing drill where the only decision to be taken was to swing the arm quickly.

It would then be built up by adding in movement and a predictable feed. This would require you to think about where the ball was coming from **and** the pace at which you have to swing your arm. Time would be available after attempting the smash to think about what went well and which decisions had been successful.

Then an unpredictable feed might be added. This adds the demand for an additional decision to be made, i.e. 'where do I need to move to on the court to hit the ball?' **and** to remember to hit the ball with a fast arm.

This series of drills would be built up by adding a little more pressure each time. The pressure would come from the **number** of decisions you were having to make and the **time** available for you to make these decisions.

The decisions might be:

GO! Activity

Describe the decisions which are being taken at each of the stages opposite.

Decision	Few decisions required	Lots of decisions required
Do I have to move to get the ball?	No – feed is coming straight to me	Yes – random, unpredictable feed
Where do I have to play the ball from on court?	I know where I will have to play the ball from	Wherever the feeder makes me play it from
Where do I need to play the ball back to?	Anywhere, no pressure to hit a target	Back to a target zone
What will happen if my return is poor?	Nothing – I will try again	The opponent will smash it back at me or I will lose a point

✔Assessment in PE

1.3 Explaining two approaches to develop performance.

2.3 Selecting and applying two approaches to impact positively on a performance.

These approaches are very personal to each performer and require that you show understanding of how concentration is linked to level of arousal and, as a consequence, to decision-making. In this way you can show how the same method can be used to improve more than one feature.

Monitoring and evaluating

Do this by retesting through the performance analysis process you completed when you began to focus on your mental factors.

The opinions of your teacher or coach and your own personal reflections on how you felt before and during the performance will often back up what your analysis process tells you.

This is a valuable process because it allows you to identify what you need to do now to keep your performance improving and if the practices you went through had a positive impact on your overall performance.

✔Assessment in PE

2.4 Monitoring and recording performance development sessions.

Your record of the progress you make while trying to develop the mental factor will provide evidence that you have achieved this assessment standard.

Future needs

Any successful training programme should include consideration of your mental fitness. Preparation before a performance should always allow you to 'think' about what you have to do, about the decisions you need to make and to focus your mind on the important aspects involved. Training should always be done to help you cut out distractions as soon as possible and to prepare the mind to play its part in a successful performance.

Check your progress

Complete the following to check your understanding of this chapter.

	HELP NEEDED	GETTING THERE	CONFIDENT
1. List the three mental features you have learned about in this chapter.	◯	◯	◯
2. Choose one feature and explain how you might collect information about how the feature impacts on performance.	◯	◯	◯
3. Choose one feature and explain how this feature impacts on your performance.	◯	◯	◯
4. Explain how you would develop this feature.	◯	◯	◯
5. Describe in detail how improved mental fitness can impact on performance.	◯	◯	◯

Make a judgement – were you able to complete these easily? If not, go back and look over some of the explanations or speak to your teacher for further advice.

SECTION 4
The social factor

7 The social factor

This chapter deals with some of the social features that have an impact on your participation within physical activity and sport.

The features we will explore are:

- Peer group influence
- Inclusion
- Etiquette
- Roles and responsibilities
- Cooperation

In this chapter you will learn:

1. How the social factor can impact on performance.
2. How to gather information by using a questionnaire and a self-appraisal checklist.
3. How to prepare for performance development by setting achievable and realistic targets.
4. To understand and apply approaches to develop performance.
5. To monitor performance using self-reflection sheets and questionnaires.
6. To identify and explain future performance development needs.

🧠 What should I already know?

Every activity you have done as part of your BGE has included consideration of the social factor. You will have been part of teams and groups where you will have had to cooperate with others to improve your performance. Your behaviour and respect for others while you participated in different activities will also have been a focus for you as you learned (HWB 4-23a).

Sport has always had a 'social' element to it. People take part in sport for a variety of reasons and have their own preferences as to which activities they prefer. History tells us that sport was an important part of culture and even today communities and countries organise their physical activities in many different ways.

The reason you choose to do the activities you do, the role you play in these activities and even your behaviour and conduct are all influenced by the experiences you have had either taking part in or watching sport.

📌 Fact

In ancient Rome, during the Olympics, men competed in the nude!

Feature of the factor: peer group influence

A peer group is a social group with common interests and backgrounds. This could be a group of friends your own age either from school or outside school.

Groups within groups can form and this sometimes causes problems or strengthens bonds between different people.

When then participating in a team or group performance, these relationships can be complex. For example, if two of the girls from within one of the groups have a disagreement it will have a negative impact on the whole group dynamic. One person might then feel isolated and as a result other friendship groups can be affected.

The size of the group can vary and the group can be made up of different personalities.

The role you have within this peer group or team will also have an impact on your performance.

Perhaps you have taken up the role of the captain or have become the organiser of performances.

Working together and showing respect for one another is crucial.

How does peer group pressure impact positively on performance?

Your peer group can influence your decisions to take part in an activity you may not have considered.

When you have a positive group of friends encouraging you to take part in something, you feel much more confident in your abilities and are more willing to participate.

This can impact positively on your performance, as you will feel part of the team or group, which will increase your motivation and determination levels.

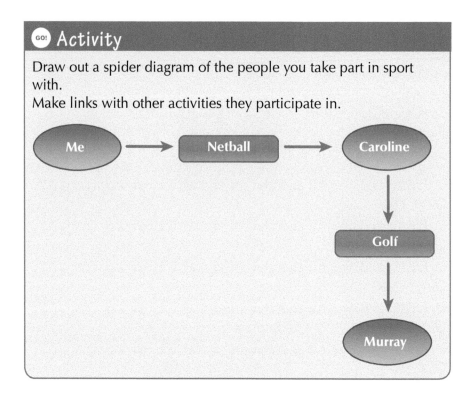

GO! Activity

Draw out a spider diagram of the people you take part in sport with.
Make links with other activities they participate in.

Within your group/team it is important that you can work and cooperate with one and other. This is of particular importance when you are deciding which role/position you are to carry out in the performance. This must be clearly defined, with all parties adopting a positive attitude and the necessary commitment to work together.

When everyone agrees on their role and understands the support they must give to one another when performing, strong positive relationships are built. These relationships become the foundation within a group or team and often when the group or team is under pressure, bonds of mutual respect and cooperation are what carry the group through to success.

For example, at a netball match one of the shooters loses confidence because of a very tall agile defender. This makes her shooting deteriorate and she begins to find it difficult to score. The rest of the team begin to encourage her and to applaud her shooting attempts. This increases her confidence and eventually she begins to score more. In this way the peer group influenced performance positively.

How does peer group influence impact negatively on performance?

Sometimes you may want to try out a new activity, but your group of friends don't seem to be interested. They may even try to put pressure on you not to try it. You may then miss out on an opportunity to try something new and exciting.

Within a team or group being unable to work together can have a negative impact on performance.

For example, in basketball if you are unable to work with others in your team, as you don't get along with some of the players, you may be unwilling to prepare yourself properly, as you feel you are not valued in the team.

During the game you feel left out, rarely get passed the ball and are criticised openly.

This will impact negatively on your performance as you will feel less confident to go for an interception and will lose your focus because of the pressure others are putting you under.

☼ CFE focus

Having respect for the members of your peer group/team and the roles and responsibilities they take on is important.

If everyone carries out their own duties to the best of their abilities then collectively, as a team or group, they are more likely to be successful.

● Make the link

Within your broad and general education at level 3 and level 4 you will have been given opportunities to develop positive relationships, where working with others will have been important.

Feature of the factor: inclusion

Everyone, no matter what their background or ability, should be able to take part in a range of activities. Ensuring that every participant, irrespective of their ability, gender or age, should have equal access to sports facilities is a major focus for both local sporting bodies and the government.

How does inclusion impact positively on performance?

Most sports facilities and certainly schools have a responsibility to make sure young people are able to have fair access to all physical activities and sports. This means that the range of activities on offer should be able to **include** everyone. This means opportunities are available for you to participate alongside others who are older or even younger than yourself or from a different cultural background where appropriate. Girls can have the chance to play in boys' football or rugby teams at certain ages or should have their own teams set up.

In dance, groups containing boys and girls have existed for many years. This means that equal opportunities for participation are available for both genders.

How does lack of inclusion impact negatively on performance?

For a disabled performer, for example, there is a need for a wheelchair hoist to get you into the swimming pool so that you can train effectively for your swim meet. Being unable to use a local pool and so having to travel to a swimming pool further away that has the hoist facility, could have a negative impact on your preparation.

If you want to play football and because your age group means you need to play in a single-sex team, you need to try to find a club that offers this facility. If there are no girls football teams where you live, then you could say that you are excluded from this opportunity.

Activity

Here is an example of how social factors can impact on your performance.

Social issue: peer group influence

None of my friends want to try the new Zumba club in the village and I don't have the confidence to go on my own.

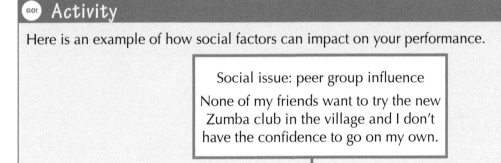

Impact

I really want to try out this new activity, but I just don't have the confidence to go on my own. I'll just have to miss out.

Impact

My friends are getting fed up of me trying to persuade them to go!

Impact

I'm never going to get any fitter.

Use the above example to complete a similar diagram to represent an aspect of your own social situation.

Think about using one of the key social features: inclusion, etiquette, roles and responsibilities, inclusion or etiquette.

Share this information with a group of your friends.

Feature of the factor: etiquette

Etiquette is sometimes referred to as the 'unwritten rules'. These are things that mean a competition or event can be conducted in good spirit and with good behaviour from all involved – performers and spectators.

There are many examples of good etiquette where players will allow their opposition time to recover after falling or being injured or when good play is applauded.

However, there are also times when bad behaviour can result in a player being cautioned by the umpire.

The etiquette of the performer can influence the etiquette of the audience, and vice versa.

How does good etiquette impact positively on performance?

Showing appropriate etiquette means a performance is likely to be good-tempered and fair.

During a golf match, for example, players allow each other to take their shots without any distractions.

This means any competition can be conducted in a straightforward way and the game is likely to be enjoyable for all.

 **Activity**

Think about and record on flip chart paper the examples you know of good and bad sporting etiquette.

GO! Activity

Complete the following table using a different activity.

Activity 1	Before the event the performer **should**	During the event the performer **should**	After the event the performer **should**
Football	Shake hands	Kick the ball out of play if a player gets injured	Shake hands
Activity 2			

How does poor etiquette impact negatively on performance?

Poor etiquette often means performance is disrupted. Players using bad language, kicking walls in frustration and even spitting on others demonstrates this.

Sometimes poor etiquette is the result of poor concentration. If concentration is lost and the focus for the performer becomes anger, frustration or upset because of a bad refereeing decision, then skill and the overall quality of the performance will deteriorate.

Skills for life, learning and work

Part of being a valuable employee will concern your ability to just 'get on with others'. This means you need to learn the skills of how to cooperate, how to compete in the correct way and how to carry out your duties or the role you are employed to fulfil.

Feature of the factor: roles and responsibilities

Often when performing you will have certain roles to perform and/or duties to carryout. In an individual activity you will be responsible for arriving at the right part of the stadium in time in order to compete in your race. In team activities you might be the person who sets up the playing area or who organises the distribution of kit. Whatever duties you have, they have an impact on your involvement in the activity. Duties are often shared out to make sure everyone feels part of the group. This develops strong positive bonds where people feel valued for their contributions. The roles and responsibilities you have within a group are often determined by the personal qualities you have, e.g. being well organised, or having a positive outlook.

How do roles and responsibilities impact positively on performance?

GO! Activity

Make a spider diagram for an activity you are familiar with, listing all the roles and responsibilities which exist.

If you feel valued within your group it means you are likely to work well within the group. You will try hard not to let the group members down and will make every effort to support other players, e.g. in the last stages of a game if you can see they are tiring. In gymnastics, you would support your partner as she comes off the box in her sequence, making sure she does not get injured.

When you understand what role you have to play in a team or group it means you are clear about what duties that role requires you to fulfil. For example, a team would be weaker if the centre midfield did not come back to cover after a run up field to help with a goal-scoring opportunity.

In volleyball the libero player understands his role is to pick up any loose balls around the middle of the court, by diving if necessary.

In doubles badminton each player must know what to do if the other is pulled into the net by a tight net shot. The cover, which should be put in place, gives the player caught out of position time to recover to the correct position.

The captain in any team must appreciate the role they have to play before, during and after the match. By encouraging others, making them feel supported and appreciated then the likelihood of a strong positive performance is more certain. Having an ethos of praise and encouragement throughout a game can mean a team will eventually overcome stronger opposition just because of a positive, determined, never-give-up attitude.

How do roles and responsibilities impact negatively on performance?

Lack of clarity about who does what in a team or group causes confusion. This means people don't know where they should be or what they should be doing. A strong opposition can quickly exploit gaps that occur as players are caught out of position.

In the basketball fast break, if the person receiving the outlet pass does not carry out their duties effectively by getting into the middle of the court quickly then the chances are the ball will be intercepted, resulting in an easy turnover.

A captain with poor leadership skills will be indecisive and uncertain and will not be able to give the appropriate advice when the team is under pressure, e.g. in the case of a penalty in football where he allows the wrong person to take the kick.

In trampolining, the performer is responsible for beginning their routine when they have achieved their preferred height of bounce. They must be able to decide at which point this happens. This gives their complete responsibility for the start of their rehearsed sequence.

Feature of the factor: cooperation

There should be a high degree of cooperation in any team or group activity. This allows for everyone to feel secure that should they make a mistake cover and consideration will be available.

A positive cooperative culture should exist, where everyone feels confident to be creative, to try and score more goals, take on more players, and that if they should fail blame and negativity will not be the result.

How does cooperation impact positively on performance?

When a positive cooperative culture exists players develop confidence and trust in one another. This leads to a healthy performance environment.

In volleyball, the spiker feels comfortable trying a tip over the block from a good set. Even if it lands out of court he will feel that it was worth trying and his team will support his decision to try something different.

In a group dance the need for cooperation is high. All members of the group must be aware of their positioning in relation to others in order to stay in time and make the dance successful.

A cooperative culture encourages a good three-point shooter to try again after missing his first attempt.

In gymnastics, the gymnast can feel safe when attempting a double somersault, knowing that the two supporters will cooperate well with each other to ensure she does not fall or land badly.

How does lack of cooperation impact negatively on performance?

It is obvious when a team is unable to cooperate enough to achieve a satisfactory performance. Passes are given away to the opposition, ineffective tackles are made, players are caught out of position and no cover is available.

Individual players within a team might even give up trying.

In volleyball the team should cooperate as a unit, constantly readjusting to cover players moving. If this does not happen then there are exposed areas for the opposition to play the ball into.

In netball morale drops as the team is being beaten. Players start to argue with each other and complain when possession is given away instead of encouraging each other to mark tightly to try to deny passing options.

How do I gather information on these features?

Questionnaire

Designing a questionnaire to look at the social reasons why you wish to take part in sport will help you to gather information on all the social features (peer group influence, inclusion, roles and responsibilities, cooperation) that impact on your participation. An example is given below.

Why do I want to be part of my local rugby team?

Place a tick in each box next to a reason/statement you agree with.

To be with my friends ☐

To meet new friends ☐

To be healthy ☐

The club is local ☐

The facilities are good ☐

I enjoy team activities ☐

I like the chance of taking some responsibility within a team ☐

I like to compete ☐

> **Make the link**
>
> You may have used questionnaires when gathering information on emotional or mental factors. You may be able to use some of the information from these questionnaires to help you with your social questionnaire.

Self-appraisal

Reflecting on the range of personal and social lifestyles (either by yourself or with a group of friends), will help you gather information on the social features which have most impact on your participation and performance. It would be a good idea to take a note of these. Use the following template and adapt it to suit your own circumstances.

Tick where appropriate	Team activities	Individual activities	Creative activities	Competitive activities
I feel I mostly like…				
My friends mostly like…				
I take part in sport or physical activity with…	My family	My friends	Other people	
I feel that …	All activities I am interested in doing are available to me	Some activities I would like to do are not available to me	Most of the activities I would like to do are not available to me	
I take part in sport or physical activity…	To be healthy	To be with my friends	Because it's part of my routine	Because I live near good facilities and clubs
My conduct when participating is…	Good – rarely cause or experience any problems	OK – sometimes I lose my temper and end up in a bad mood because we lose		Poor – I have been sent off or cautioned by the officials because of my conduct
I like having a role of responsibility within a group or team	Yes	No		

Once you have completed this appraisal sheet you can begin to see the social features that are important to you when taking part in physical activity and sport.

You should now try to draw a personal profile graphic organiser of your preferences (things you have highlighted as liking) and also of areas you might like to investigate further.

Personal profile graphic organiser

Another method of gathering information on your behaviour or conduct within a performance would be your **discipline/foul record**. In any sporting performance, records of behaviour and fouls will be held. It may be possible to look back and gain information over a period of time. This would give you a clear indication of your conduct while participating.

Gathering evidence relating to etiquette would be an unusual course of action. However, within class competition or events it might be something you decide to focus on. This involves drawing up a list of behaviours you want each person to use, e.g. shaking hands before beginning, finding out the opponent's name, acknowledging a good shot or apologising for a shot which accidentally hit the opponent. In this way you are deciding the criteria you want demonstrated in terms of good etiquette. You could use these criteria to draw up a checklist relating to etiquette. For example:

Activity: netball		
Name of player………………………………………………..		
Etiquette to be shown	YES	NO
Shake hands with opponent before starting		
Introduce yourself – give your name		
Say – good luck, play well		
Do not speak back to the umpire		
Apologise if you make contact		
Shake hands at the end		
Thank the umpire		

GO! Activity

Choose another activity and draw up a checklist of etiquette you would want to be displayed.

☑Assessment in PE

1.1 Explaining in detail two methods used to identify factors impacting on performance.

These methods could be explained to show how you found out information about the impact social factors have on performance.

Preparation for performance development

You must identify the main social feature that has an impact on your ability to be an effective part of an activity and clearly set out steps that you will need to take in order to meet your goals. By setting goals you can focus on specific areas of this social factor and the influence it has on your overall performance.

Approaches that impact positively on performance

If your peer group is holding you back from effective participation it could be for any number of reasons. However, you need to identify what you want to be able to do and if your friendship groups are unwilling to join you then you should feel secure knowing you are right to be independent and stay determined to join the activity with or without them. You could also reassure your friends that you will still make time for them and that your strong bonds will remain.

If within a team or group who are performing together there are negative peer group influences, then a coach or teacher might want to set up some **team-building approaches** to improve the relationships within the group.

This approach often starts with fun, easy activities intended to get everyone relaxed and open to communicate with each other.

One activity that might be used to begin this training is to use a ball and as everyone throws it around the circle they firstly call out their own name, then they call out the name of someone they are going to pass to. This exercise gets people to think, to make eye contact and to relax.

From here the group would be set a task that they must achieve together or in smaller sub-groups. A wise leader would set the groups up carefully to make sure the people who struggle to get on with others are working with other people who will try to include them in the problem-solving activity.

By working through a problem together, positive relationships can be established. This new positivity should be carried back over into the game/performance situation.

This team building could become a strong feature of your team/ group training. The aim is to build stronger positive relationships to ensure negative behaviour (which might exclude others) is minimised.

GO! Activity

Activity: hockey
Team-building task 1
As quickly as possible, rearrange the hockey sticks to make the name of someone in your team.
Team-building task 2
Discuss with your team one unusual attack sequence that could be used to win a point in a game.
Activity: Dance
Team-building task 3
Every person has to add one motif to a sequence for a dance. All of these should be joined together to form one sequence.

1 - - - ➤ 2 - - - ➤ 3 - - - ➤ 4 - - - ➤ 5 - - - ➤

GO! Activity

Following your next performance, ask an observer to use the 'praise sandwich' approach. Think and record in your personal reflections diary about how the feedback made you feel.

GO! Activity

Make a list of other team-building activities you could organise to build positive peer group relationships.

The praise sandwich

Team-building tasks build in **positive reinforcement** to foster good, strong, positive relationships within the group. This is where feedback is delivered using first some positive statement followed by negative (but constructive) feedback and finally by another piece of positive feedback. This is sometimes called a 'praise sandwich' and it makes the person in receipt of the feedback feel there are at least some positives in their performance. By insisting praise is used effectively when completing tasks in practice, morale is built and group members feel valued and involved in decisions, discussions and plans that will be used in the performance setting.

Cooperation

To build **cooperation**, the same type of team-building activities could be organised where the focus is on finding solutions to problems together in a group.

By structuring activities that enable everyone to contribute, cooperation grows. An old saying that 'a team is only as strong as its weakest player' is a very good way to look at cooperation.

When using the team-building approach to encourage cooperation, everyone should have a chance to be involved in how the problem might be solved. In this way everyone feels valued and experiences the success of solving a problem together with others.

Communication

In terms of using approaches to impact on understanding of the **roles and responsibilities** a performer has, good communication routines is a very useful and straightforward approach to use.

Teams and groups use quite structured ways of making sure everyone understands what each person must do in a performance situation.

A hockey team would sit in the dressing room and listen to the coach explaining what everyone has to do in terms of defence and attack. Particular players might be given additional duties in terms of marking one or two specific players from the opposition and the captains would obviously have their role outlined again so that every player knows who is in charge on the pitch. This is probably the same in all team sports.

Etiquette

Etiquette is not a usual area a performer would be concerned with and so approaches used to develop this feature would only be by **using positive role models** who demonstrate and are admired for their fair play and sportsmanship. Sometimes games or competitions include a reward for the player who demonstrates this feature in order to reinforce the fact that **everyone** should show respect for one another.

Inclusion

To impact positively on inclusion it would be necessary to find out who you could contact to increase the opportunities for activities you feel are not accessible to you. There are local government bodies who have a responsibility to respond to requests for new activities, facilities or additional support for young people wanting to take part in sport or physical activity.

☑ Assessment in PE

2.2 Preparing and implementing a personal development plan containing clearly identified development targets.

By using, for example, the team-building approach you should able to put in place and explain how you used the programme of work to have a positive impact on the peer group relationships within your team or group. This would also let you work towards achieving the assessment standard:

1.2 Explaining two approaches to develop performance.

Monitoring and evaluating

Again, a training diary can help you keep a note of the progress you are making while trying to deal with issues arising from the social factor. Look at Chapter 8 to see a template you could use.

Future needs

This area of your performance is another area that will probably be an ongoing focus for you while performing. In this way you will remain aware of the effects of peer groups within your team or group and the need to cooperate and fulfil your duties effectively and in a fair and mature way.

Check your progress

Complete the following to check your understanding.

	HELP NEEDED	GETTING THERE	CONFIDENT
1. What are the types of social features you might consider to help you improve your performance?	◯	◯	◯
2. How would you gather information on these social features?	◯	◯	◯
3. Who might you want to involve?	◯	◯	◯
4. What are the barriers when considering the impact of social factors?	◯	◯	◯

Make a judgement – were you able to complete these easily? If not, go back and look over some of the explanations or speak to your teacher for further advice.

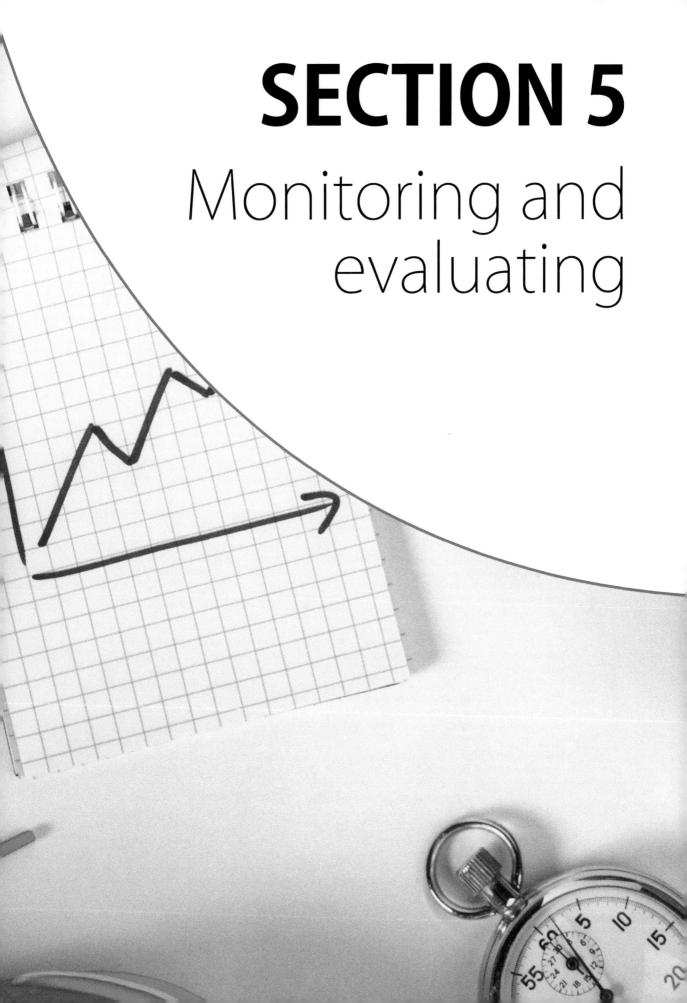

SECTION 5
Monitoring and evaluating

8 Monitoring and evaluating

In order to continue to improve the impact that factors will have on your performance, you must consider how you will monitor and evaluate your performance and the performance development process.

The process of monitoring occurs **while** you are training and evaluation **after** you finish training.

The evaluation is concerned with whether the training you planned and put in place actually worked. This process always involves revisiting your original methods of collecting data on your whole performance.

One method you may wish to consider is keeping a **personal** reflections diary to monitor the progress you make during your approaches to performance development. You can use a diary for all four factors.

The table below gives you some extracts from a diary on the different factors impacting on performance.

		Extract from diary
Physical	Consider your own personal reflections on how you felt before and during the performance in relation to the physical factor. For fitness you may wish to consider writing up information on your progress with any of the training approaches. Have you been challenged? Is it too easy? Were you always motivated?	'My first training session went well. I felt I was able to cope with the demands of the interval training and found this quite exciting. Next session I am going to consider how to make this harder.'
	Consider your own personal reflections on how you felt before and during the performance in relation to the physical factor. For skills you may wish to consider writing up information on your progress with any of the training approaches. Have you highlighted the parts of the skill you are weak at? Have you been able to record whether any improvement has been made or not?	'Tuesday 6 June badminton session – trained for 40 minutes. Repeated observation schedules, which showed me that I still need to work on my smash and my transfer of weight. Set up a feeder practice to mid court, which allowed me to concentrate on transferring my weight. This seemed to work well, as it highlighted the problem. Had a little more success with my smash in a half court game.'
	Consider your own personal reflections on how you felt before and during the performance in relation to the physical factor. For tactics and composition you may wish to consider whether the selected SFC was successful or not. Did all the individuals carry out their roles correctly? What feedback did you receive from your coach/ teacher?	'During our performance against a team we lost to last time we played them, changing our formation to a zone defence really allowed us to keep our opponents out of the key. We were then able to counter-attack and score more unopposed baskets.'

(continued)

			Extract from diary
Emotional	Consider your own personal reflections on how you felt before and during the performance in relation to the emotional factor.		*'When I was preparing for my dance performance, I found I became quite anxious before presenting.'*
Mental	Consider your own personal reflections on how you felt before and during the performance in relation to the mental factor.		*'During my performance I felt I lost my concentration, especially when my team started to concede goals.'*
Social	Consider your own personal reflections on how you felt before and during the performance in relation to the social factor. In your diary you may wish to consider: How well do you work with others? Have you been able to join a new club? Have you been able to persuade any of your friends to become involved?		*'During my planning and performance I reflected how well I got on with the rest of my teammates during our netball game. I felt I was able to listen and work well with others initially, then on occasions I stepped back and was less involved in some parts of the game.'*

Completing a form of analysis during your performance, then comparing and contrasting to the result of other performances, will help you monitor the progress you are making.

Methods of monitoring performance

You may wish to consider other methods for monitoring performance. Some of the methods we have discussed in this book are outlined in the table below.

General observation schedule	Focused observation schedule	Scatter diagram
Digital analysis	Coach feedback	Knowledge of results
Skills test	Personal reflection	Training diary card
Match analysis	Fitness tests	Score sheet

For example, in your physical factor you may have been working on improving your fitness levels. By repeating fitness tests you should be able to see improvements in your scores. This would indicate whether your particular aspect of fitness had improved or not. Remember to make sure you carry out the test under the same conditions.

A circuit training card keeps a record of the number of repetitions, sets and stations you complete during each training session. Each time you do this training the card must be completed. This gives a permanent record of the work you do and the progress you make using this method of training. This allows you to monitor the progress you are making and to ensure that session-to-session and week-to-week you are increasing the amount of work you do to make sure your performance continually improves. Here is an example of a circuit training card.

Local muscular endurance circuit card			
Activity: netball	Area of focus: arms, shoulders and legs		
Station	Maximum in 1 minute	Training load (50% of maximum)	
1. Step-ups			
2. Chest passes			
3. Sergeant jumps			
4. Press-ups			
5. Overhead medicine ball throw			
6. Squat thrusts			
Week 1	Session 1 Time taken	Session 2 Time taken	Session 3 Time taken
3 sets of 6 stations at 50% of maximum			
Week 2	Session 1 Time taken	Session 2 Time taken	Session 3 Time taken
3 sets of 6 stations with 4 reps added to each			
Week 3	Session 1 Time taken	Session 2 Time taken	Session 3 Time taken
4 sets of each station with same number of reps as week 2			

The latest technology in electronic data collection is now widely available.

You might want to investigate the range of apps you could use e.g. paceTracker to monitor the work you complete and the targets you set yourself for improvement.

Training diary

Here is an example of a training diary for a hockey player. Use the headings to make up your own diary.

Date	Time	Description of training completed	Feelings during and after training	Next steps/plan for next session
EXAMPLE 3 June	7.20 pm	Warm up – gentle jog for 8 mins, 10 mins of stretching. 35 mins Fartlek training session. Used short sides of hockey pitch to sprint. Jogged all long sides. Replaced sprints on last lap with 2 jogs. Warm down walking for 8 mins and gentle stretching for 10 mins	Felt very good at the beginning, felt able to really push myself at the sprints and that I had recovered enough by the time I had to sprint again. Near the end got a bit bored and felt I couldn't complete the last 2 sprints.	Repeat the session, try to complete all sprints.

Score sheets

Here is an example of a score sheet in basketball. How could you use this to monitor your performance?

Competition _Champions Cup_   **Time** _18.30_ **Date** _30/01/14_ **Match No** _023_

Hamilton Hawks   v   _Carnoustie Cougars_

Venue _EM Arena_   **Referee** _K. Power_   **Umpire 1** _C. Lamb_   **Umpire 2** _G. Munter_

FIRST HALF SCORE   **SECOND HALF SCORE**   **EXTRA PERIODS SCORE**

Team A: _Hamilton Hawks_

Colour: _Red_

Team Fouls Period ○☐☐☐☐ ○☐☐☐☐
○☐☐☐☐ ○☐☐☐☐

Time-outs
Period ○ & ○☐☐ ○ & ○☐☐ Extra ☐☐

Licence No.	Players		Fouls 1 2 3 4 5
420	C. Balfour		
432	M. Brown		
418	S. Neville		
412	G. Stewart		
425	S. Loose		
428	A. Agnew		
441	D. Anderson		
421	D. Marshall		
412	C. Ryce		
409	A. Gupwell		
407	A. McKechnie		
411	D. Pollock		
450	Coach: R. Leckie		
460	Assistant coach: S. Gow		

Team B: _Carnoustie Cougars_

Colour: _Blue_

Team Fouls Period ○☐☐☐☐ ○☐☐☐☐
○☐☐☐☐ ○☐☐☐☐

Time-outs
Period ○ & ○☐☐ ○ & ○☐☐ Extra ☐☐

Licence No.	Players		Fouls 1 2 3 4 5
704	J. Donnelly		
711	K. Byrne		
708	R. Campbell		
721	D. Austin		
709	K. Bradshaw		
718	D. Reid		
712	C. McBain		
732	A. Smith		
738	C. Potter		
739	N. Allan		
725	K. Dean		
713	K. Bell		
750	Coach: S. Mitchell		
760	Assistant coach: V. Alexander		

		Name	Signature
Referee	2002	K. POWER	K. Power
Umpire 1	2009	C. LAMB	c.lamb
Umpire 2	2010	G. MUNTER	G.Munter
Scorer	2058	K. MOORE	keith moore
Timekeeper	2062	S. WOODS	S.WOODS
24s Operator	2069	K. ROBBINS	KRobbins

Scores: Period A____ B____   A____ B____
Period A____ B____   A____ B____
Extra Periods A____   B____

Final Score: Team A____   Team B____

Name of winning team

ORGANISER'S COPY

Feedback

The opinions of your teacher or coach and your own personal reflections on how you felt before and during the performance will often back up what your development process has told you.

Your own reflections can be recorded in a personal reflections diary, like the example below.

Type of competition	Venue	Date	Audience	Observations about my level of arousal before and during performance

Whatever methods you use to gather information on your performance will include feedback from others. Indeed you might on occasion be the person giving feedback to a partner who has just finished a sequence. You must be willing to take on board the feedback given and to use it to help develop your performance further.

Evaluating your performance

The evaluation of how effective your approaches have been should be a straightforward comparison between what your performance was before you started training and what it is after completing after training.

The table below highlights some possible evaluations within each factor.

Factor	Methods of monitoring	Evaluation of performance
Mental	Personal reflection before and after developing approaches	I now feel I have much more focus during my performance. I am able to concentrate throughout, even when there are distractions.
Emotional	Questionnaire	I am now losing control of my temper less and feeling less frightened or feeling more confident. My mental rehearsal approach has had a positive impact on my overall performance, as I am now able to focus more on improving my skill level in my performance.
Social	Checklist	I can now see that I am much better at working with others. I am happy to take a leading role, as well as to listen to others.
Physical-fitness	Sit and reach test	After I developed my flexibility, my pike position in trampolining is more effective.
Physical-skills	Scatter diagram – before and end of programme	I can now consistently play a backhand drive. This has had a positive impact on my tennis performance, as I am able to return the ball more effectively.
Physical – SFC	Diary	From the information in my diary I can see that during my fast break I am now moving much quicker and making the correct decisions.

GO! Activity

Get a coach/partner/observer to complete the second version of your whole performance analysis and compare the two records.

What changes can you see in your performance?
Record them in the following table:

Before training I was able to:	After training I am able to:
E.g. play accurate passes until around 70 minutes into the game	E.g. keep the accuracy of my passing high throughout the whole match

The benefits of monitoring and evaluating

- To help with your own motivation and desire to improve.
- To help with forward planning.
- To see whether the approaches you have used have been suitable, challenging and successful.
- To allow you to make changes to your approaches.
- To make comparisons.
- To see whether you have met your development needs.
- To help you identify future development needs.

◈ CfE focus

Seeing the benefit of this ongoing training cycle and taking responsibility for being determined to continue to improve is part of being a **successful learner**. By monitoring closely the progress you make and the steps you need to take to keep improving, you will develop skills of self-regulation and self-discipline. These will help keep you healthy all through your life.

Future needs

Following your process of monitoring and evaluating the success of your approaches to development, you may be able to identify next steps or future needs.

By retesting and evaluating the process you have completed you will be able to identify any features within the factors that still require focus. By then attempting to modify what you did to further improve your performance, future needs can be addressed.

You may decide to:

- Continue to work on the same factor.
- Change to another factor or particular feature of that factor.

The identification of future needs is an important part of performance development. This allows you to reflect on what has gone well, the progress you have made and the areas of your performance that still require attention.

✔ Assessment in PE

2.4 Monitoring and recording performance development sessions.

3.1 Seeking feedback from others.

3.2 Evaluating the effectiveness of the personal development plan in supporting performance development.

3.3 Evaluating progress based on all information gathered.

3.4 Identifying and explaining future development needs.

You may wish to consider some of the features above to help you gather evidence to link to the assessment standard for 'monitoring, recording and evaluating performance development' in your portfolio.

Inventory of all methods of data collection

Method	Area tested
General observation schedule	Various
PAR sheet	Skill
Scatter diagram	Skill
Calculation app	Distance covered and average speed
Scatter diagram app	Skill
Cooper test	CRE
Leger test	CRE
Ruler drop test	Reaction time
Sit and reach test	Flexibility
Groin stretch test	Flexibility
Illinois test	Agility
T test	Agility
Sprint test	Speed
Plate tapping	Coordination
Alternative hand ball throw test	Coordination
Maximum in 1 minute test	LME
POOCH	Various
Graphic organisers	Various
Performance timeline	CRE

Approaches to develop performance

Approach	Used to develop
Stretching	Flexibility
Circuits	Agility, LME
Interval training	Speed and CRE
Continuous running, cycling or swimming	CRE
Conditioning	CRE and skills
Weights and resistance training	Strength
Positive self-talk	Mental and emotional features
Rehearsal	Mental and emotional features
Visualisation	Mental and emotional features
Shadowing	Skill
Repetition drills	Skill
Pressure drills	Skill
Conditioned games	Skill
Passive defence drills	Strategies
Active defence drills	Strategies
Gradual build up (GBU)	Skills
Whole-part-whole (WPW)	Skills
Team-building	Positive peer-group dynamics and cooperation
Positive reinforcement	Positive team relationships and cooperation
Communication	Understanding of roles and responsibilities
Use of positive role models	Etiquette

Methods of monitoring performance development

Method	Used to monitor
Training diary	All
Personal reflections diary	All
Pacetracker/Runkeeper app	Physical fitness